101 Fabulous
Dairy-free
Desserts
Everyone Will Love

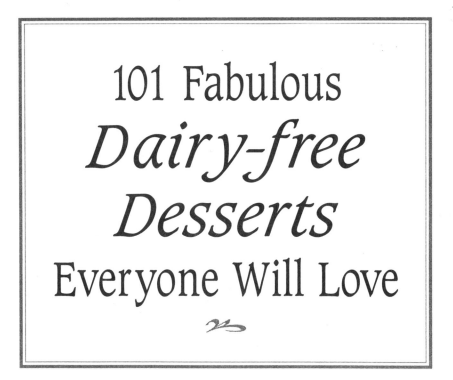

101 Fabulous
Dairy-free Desserts
Everyone Will Love

For the lactose intolerant, the dairy allergic,
and their friends and families

Annette Pia Hall

STATION HILL OPENINGS
BARRYTOWN, LTD.

Published by Barrytown, Ltd. Barrytown, New York 12507, under Station Hill Openings imprint.

Web: www.stationhill.org
E-mail: publishers@stationhill.org

Cover and text design by Susan Quasha
Photographs by C. Vaughan Seifert

Library of Congress Cataloging-in-Publication Data

Hall, Annette Pia.
    101 fabulous dairy free desserts everyone will love : for the lactose-intolerant, the dairy-allergic, and their friends and families / Annette Pia Hall.
      p. cm.
    ISBN 1-58177-018-9 (alk. paper)
    1. Desserts. 2. Milk-free diet—Recipes. 3. Lactose intolerance—Diet therapy—Recipes. I. Title. II. Title: One hundred one fabulous dairy free desserts everyone will love.   III. Title: One hundred and one fabulous dairy free desserts everyone will love.
TX773.H245 1998
641.8'6—dc21   97-35372
                                               CIP

Contents

III COOKIES & CANDIES

IV MUFFINS & BREADS

V   PIES & TARTS & COBBLERS

Mutti and Vati
This book is dedicated to you.
Thank you for giving me the confidence
to accomplish whatever I set out to do
and for giving me free reign in your kitchen
from the time I was a little girl.

Acknowledgements

Special thanks to the many people who, throughout the years, have tested my recipes and supported me with their good wishes, active interest and near perfect attendance at my dessert parties: my husband Vaughan, my son Stefan, my daughter Elise, my parents Ed and Anneliese Hall, my sister Karen Hall, Peggy Jensen, Aunt Maggie and Uncle Joe Osgood, Mary Lou and Jay Altman, Greg Dondero, Deirdre Sullivan and Patrick Hart, Carole Ann Saracco and Tom McFadden, Donald Seifert and Lorise Van Voorthuizen, Steve Quezada and Chris Sutherland, our nanny and friend Carol Lewicki and her entire family, Mel Hartley, Dave and Emily Lengyel, Liz Haggerty, Judy Hummel, Penny Fink, Steve Figman, Steven Maskar, The Lindgrens, The Ameses, the Dawsons, Mrs. Markiewicz, Jim and Grace Meyer, The Racines, Cathy Hammond, Beth Dwyer, Sandy, Nate and Gladys Altman, Lynn Gruss, Nancy Hill and Jay Moses, Nancy and Dick Horsfield, my friends and co-workers at Filene's in Boston, Mass., Jeffrey Kruskall, Jeff Zunick, John Marconi, Patti Gregory, Mike Beaudoin, Laura Prewitt, Brian Cope, Kim Lancilotti, Ann Henderson, David Triompo, Bob Bernard, Rich Wilson, Carolyn Smith and Marie Fratto, to mention only a few, and Mrs. Germain, my daughter's second grade teacher. Special thanks to Roger and Mary Wright for the use of their photo equipment. Thanks to Foxboro Photo for developing countless rolls of film on short notice.

And last but not least, my gratitude to my Publisher, especially Susan Quasha for her creativity and elegance and to Chuck Stein for his understanding of and faith in this project.

Author's Note

Around the winter holidays I have always thrown dessert parties. It was the best way to have a lot of people over and still enjoy the party myself. The first holiday after I met Vaughan, who is severely lactose intolerant, I was in quite a dilemma. I had absolutely no desserts without milk or butter, nor could I find any recipes that sounded any good at all. My only alternative was to make up my own, so I did. The results were delicious. I only told Vaughan which desserts were lactose free and hoped my other guests would like them. They were the hit of the party!

Throughout the next year, I developed more and more lactose-free desserts. I figured out how to make a moist yellow cake so that Vaughan could have a Boston Cream Pie. I experimented with custards so that he could enjoy an English Trifle. By the following holiday season I had so many dairy-free desserts that the whole party was dairy-free. All of my guests loved them, and they had no idea that they were enjoying desserts made without any milk, butter, cheese, cream or margarine.

Over the past few years, my husband and I have examined every lactose-free recipe we could find, but none has satisfied our discriminating palettes. A quick check on the Internet revealed that we were not the only ones in search of good lactose-free cookbooks. One site actually begged for *any* good dairy-free recipe. So, quite simply, I decided to write up my own!

Your new cookbook is full of recipes that everyone, including your lactose-intolerant or milk-allergic friends and family will love. I have personally developed, written and tested each recipe to make sure that they are easy to follow and that the results will be extremely delicious. I was careful to choose ingredients found in any supermarket. You don't have to be a master baker, you don't need a baker's kitchen—you only need to follow the directions, and you can make 101 delicious dairy-free desserts that **everyone** will love.

A Note on Lactose Intolerance and Milk Allergy

An estimated 50 million Americans are lactose intolerant—one in every five people or one in every household! In some ethnic groups the rate of adult intolerance is almost 100%.

Lactose intolerance is a simple condition, not a disease. It is the inability to digest lactose: milk sugar. To digest lactose, the body must produce the digestive enzyme, lactase. When one's digestive system produces less lactase than required to digest the lactose consumed, the symptoms of lactose intolerance appear. These symptoms are a result of the fermentation (instead of the digestion) of lactose. Fermentation produces various toxins and gasses that damage the delicate tissues of the digestive system.

Symptoms can vary widely—from mild discomfort to severe abdominal pain—depending upon how much lactose has been consumed, one's level of lactase production, the time of day, what else was eaten with the lactose-laden food, and other factors. Because the symptopms vary in intensity, lactose intolerance may easily go undetected. Sometimes one may eat lactose rich foods without problems and sometimes not.

The problem of lactose intolerance is compounded by "hidden lactose" which is prevalent in many pre-processed foods. The ingredient whey (a by-product of cheese manufacturing) is loaded with lactose. It is sweet and inexpensive and used in an astonishing array of pre-processed foods. Most cookies, breads, cereals, salad dressings, mixes, margarine and store-bought baked goods contain whey. It is even used in many prescription pills as a filler.

Milk allergy is not the same as lactose intolerance. It is an allergic response to milk, milk allergens or other allergens present in milk. This response can take many forms, some similar to lactose intolerance symptoms. Allergic reactions can also range from mild to life-threatening.

If you are a lactose intolerant or milk-allergic individual, you should be reading the label on all the packaged food you buy. If it says: milk, skim milk, lactose, whey, curds, milk by-products, dry milk solids, milk powder, cheese, sour cream, butter, butterfat, anhydrous butter, cream, buttermilk, yogurt or *any* ingredient (or by-product of any ingredient) which originated in the mammary gland of *any* mammal–don't buy it! (This includes, for example, tiger's milk or goat's milk.)

Some lactose intolerant individuals can take lactase supplements to enable them to eat dairy products. No milk-allergic person has this choice. The best approach for both is to avoid all dairy foods and all foods containing lactose.

This cookbook is in fact for everyone. Increased intolerance to dairy foods is normal for all of us as we get older: the production of lactase enzyme declines with age, so avoiding dairy products is a good idea for all adults. This should neither alarm nor depress us. As a user of this cookbook you will discover–foods without dairy products make fabulous eating!

A Note on Egg Substitutes

"Egg Beaters" may be substituted whenever whole eggs are called for in a baked dessert. The consistency of the dessert will differ from the original recipe. The substitution will not work for custards, puddings or mousse recipes.

I

Brownies
&
Squares

Mrs. Lewicki's
Apple Squares

Ingredients

4 medium sized apples, peeled, cored and cut into
  ¼-inch slices
2 cups unbleached white flour
1 teaspoon baking powder
1 teaspoon cinnamon
1 pinch salt
1 cup canola oil
1½ cups granulated sugar
1 teaspoon vanilla extract
3 large eggs, at room temperature

12-16 SQUARES

Mrs. Lewicki's Apple Squares

Directions

1. Preheat oven to 350 degrees F.
2. Lightly grease a 9x13x2-inch baking pan with canola oil.
3. Combine the flour, baking powder, cinnamon and salt. Set aside.
4. Blend the oil, sugar and vanilla together with an electric mixer on medium speed.
5. Add the eggs, one at a time, on low speed until blended.
6. Using a wooden spoon, fold in the prepared apple slices.
7. Pour the batter into the prepared pan. Bake for 40 minutes at 350 degrees F. Top will be golden brown.
8. Cool completely on a wire rack before cutting into squares and removing from the pan.

Better 'n Granny's Brownies

Ingredients

3½ ounces unsweetened chocolate
¾ cup canola oil
1½ cups granulated sugar
1 teaspoon vanilla extract
3 large eggs, at room temperature
1 cup unbleached white flour
¾ chopped nuts

12-16 BROWNIES

Better 'n Granny's Brownies

Directions

1. Preheat oven to 350 degrees F.

2. Lightly grease an 8-inch square baking pan with canola oil.

3. Melt the chocolate in a double boiler with the oil. Stir until blended. Remove from heat.

4. Blend the chocolate mixture, sugar and vanilla together with an electric mixer on medium speed.

5. Add the eggs, one at a time, on low speed until blended.

6. Gradually add the flour on low speed until completely blended.

7. Using a wooden spoon, fold in the nuts.

8. Pour the batter into the prepared pan. Bake for 40 minutes at 350 degrees F.

9. Cool on a wire rack for 1 hour before cutting into squares and removing from the pan.

10. These brownies are best eaten the day after they are baked.

Cherry Chocolate Chip Blondies

Ingredients

2¼ cups unbleached white flour
1 teaspoon baking powder
½ teaspoon baking soda
1 pinch salt
½ cup canola oil
⅔ cup light brown sugar *(lightly packed)*
½ cup granulated sugar
2 large eggs, at room temperature
1½ teaspoons almond extract
1 cup canned sour cherries, drained
9 ounces semisweet chocolate chips
½ cup chopped cashews

Important: Be sure to read the ingredients list on semisweet chocolate chips. Do not use brands that have butter fat, anhydrous butter, whey, lactose or any other dairy product.

16-20 SQUARES

Cherry Chocolate Chip Blondies

Directions

1. Preheat oven to 350 degrees F.
2. Lightly grease a 9-inch square baking pan with canola oil.
3. Combine the flour, baking powder, baking soda and salt. Set aside.
4. Blend the oil and both sugars together with an electric mixer on medium speed.
5. Add the eggs, one at a time, on medium speed until blended.
6. Add the almond extract on medium speed until blended.
7. Gradually add the flour mixture on low speed until blended.
8. Using a wooden spoon fold in the cherries, chocolate chips and nuts.
9. Pour the batter into the prepared pan. Bake for 50 minutes at 350 degrees F. Top will be golden brown. Squares will pull away from the sides.
10. Cool completely on a wire rack before cutting into squares and removing from the pan.

Chocolate Peanut Butter Brownies

Ingredients

2 ounces unsweetened chocolate

¼ cup dark corn syrup

1 tablespoon water

¾ cup unbleached white flour

1 tablespoon unsweetened cocoa

1 pinch salt

¼ teaspoon baking soda

¾ cup granulated sugar

¼ cup peanut butter

2 large egg whites, at room temperature

1 tablespoon vanilla extract

12-16 BROWNIES

Chocolate Peanut Butter Brownies

Directions

~◆~

1. Preheat oven to 350 degrees F.
2. Lightly grease an 8-inch square baking pan with canola oil.
3. Melt the chocolate in a double boiler with the corn syrup and water. Stir until blended. Remove from heat and let sit for 10 minutes.
4. Combine the flour, cocoa, salt and baking soda. Set aside.
5. Blend the chocolate mixture, sugar, peanut butter, egg whites and vanilla together with an electric mixer on low speed until smooth.
6. Gradually add the flour mixture on low speed until completely blended.
7. Pour the batter into the prepared pan. Bake for 18 minutes at 350 degrees F.
   DO NOT OVER BAKE.
8. Cool completely on a wire rack before cutting into squares and removing from the pan.

Chocolate Raspberry Squares with Almonds

Ingredients

1 ounce semisweet chocolate

3 ounces unsweetened chocolate

½ cup canola oil

1 cup unbleached white flour

½ teaspoon baking powder

2 large eggs, at room temperature

1 cup granulated sugar

1 teaspoon vanilla extract

½ cup raspberry preserves

1 cup sliced almonds *(for topping)*

Important: Be sure to read the ingredients list on semisweet chocolate chips. Do not use brands that have butter fat, anhydrous butter, whey, lactose or any other dairy product.

12 SQUARES

Chocolate Raspberry Squares with Almonds

Directions

1. Preheat oven to 350 degrees F.
2. Lightly grease a 9-inch square baking pan with canola oil.
3. Melt the chocolates in a double boiler with the oil. Stir until blended. Remove from heat.
4. Combine the flour and baking powder. Set aside.
5. Blend the eggs and sugar together with an electric mixer on medium speed until thick and light in color (about 5 minutes).
6. Add the chocolate mixture and vanilla on low speed until blended.
7. Gradually add the flour mixture on low speed until blended. **DO NOT OVER MIX.**
8. Pour the batter into the prepared pan. Bake for 20-25 minutes at 350 degrees F.
9. Allow the cake to cool for 15 minutes on a wire rack before spreading the raspberry preserves over the top.
10. Sprinkle with almonds.
11. Cut into squares while still warm but cool completely on a wire rack before removing from the pan.

Congo Squares

Ingredients

2¾ cups unbleached white flour
2½ teaspoons baking powder
1 pinch salt
¾ cup canola oil
2½ cups light brown sugar *(firmly packed)*
3 large eggs, at room temperature
2 teaspoons vanilla extract
1½ cups semisweet chocolate chips
1½ cups chopped cashews

Important: Be sure to read the ingredients list on semisweet chocolate chips. Do not use brands that have butter fat, anhydrous butter, whey, lactose or any other dairy product.

36-48 SQUARES

Congo Squares

Directions

1. Preheat oven to 350 degrees F.
2. Lightly grease an 11x9x2-inch baking pan with canola oil.
3. Combine the flour, baking powder and salt. Set aside.
4. Blend the oil and sugar together with an electric mixer on medium speed.
5. Add the eggs, one at a time, on medium speed until blended.
6. Add the vanilla on medium speed until blended.
7. Gradually add the flour mixture on low speed until blended.
8. Using a wooden spoon, fold in the chocolate chips and nuts.
9. Pour the batter into the prepared pan. Bake for 35-40 minutes at 350 degrees F. Top will be golden brown. Squares will pull away from the sides.
10. Cool completely on a wire rack before cutting into squares and removing from the pan.

Double Dutch Chocolate Brownies

Ingredients

1 ounce semisweet chocolate
2 ounces unsweetened chocolate
½ cup canola oil
1 cup granulated sugar
½ teaspoon vanilla extract
3 large eggs, at room temperature
¾ cup unbleached white flour
½ cup chopped cashews
1 cup semisweet chocolate chips

Important: Be sure to read the ingredients list on semisweet chocolate chips. Do not use brands that have butter fat, anhydrous butter, whey, lactose or any other dairy product.

12-16 BROWNIES

Double Dutch Chocolate Brownies

Directions

1. Preheat oven to 350 degrees F.
2. Lightly grease an 8-inch square baking pan with canola oil.
3. Melt 1 ounce of semisweet chocolate and 2 ounces of unsweetened chocolate in a double boiler with the oil. Stir until blended. Remove from heat and let sit for 5 minutes.
4. Blend the chocolate mixture, sugar and vanilla together with an electric mixer on medium speed.
5. Add the eggs, one at a time, on medium-low speed until blended.
6. Blend on medium speed until mixture is smooth.
7. Gradually add the flour on low speed until completely blended.
8. Using a wooden spoon, fold in the nuts and chocolate chips.
9. Pour the batter into the prepared pan. Bake for 25-30 minutes at 350 degrees F.
10. Cool on a wire rack for 1 hour before cutting into squares and removing from the pan.

Fudge Brownies

Ingredients

5 ounces unsweetened chocolate
¾ cup canola oil
2 cups granulated sugar
4 large eggs, at room temperature
1 cup unbleached white flour

16-24 SQUARES

Fudge Brownies

Directions

1. Preheat oven to 325 degrees F.

2. Lightly grease a 9-inch square baking pan with canola oil.

3. Melt the chocolate in a double boiler with the oil. Stir until blended. Remove from heat and let sit for 5 minutes.

4. Blend the sugar and eggs together with an electric mixer on medium speed.

5. Using a spatula, fold in the cooled chocolate.

6. Using a spatula, gently fold in the flour.
   DO NOT OVER MIX.

7. Pour the batter into the prepared pan. Bake for 50 minutes at 325 degrees F. Top will look dry and feel firm to the touch.

8. Cut into squares while still hot. The brownies will not look completely baked.

9. Cool on a wire rack for 1 hour before removing from the pan.

Fudge Glazed Brownies

Ingredients

BROWNIE

10 ounces bittersweet chocolate

¼ cup canola oil

½ cup light brown sugar *(lightly packed)*

½ cup granulated sugar

2 large eggs, at room temperature

1 teaspoon vanilla extract

½ cup unbleached white flour

¾ cup chopped cashews

5 ounces semisweet chocolate chips

GLAZE

6 ounces semisweet chocolate

¼ cup canola oil

2 tablespoons light corn syrup

1 teaspoon instant coffee granules

2 teaspoons vanilla extract

Important: Be sure to read the ingredients list on semisweet chocolate chips. Do not use brands that have butter fat, anhydrous butter, whey, lactose or any other dairy product.

12-16 BROWNIES

Fudge Glazed Brownies

Directions

BROWNIES

1. Preheat oven to 350 degrees F.
2. Line the bottom of a 9-inch square baking pan with wax paper cut to fit the bottom of the pan. Lightly grease with canola oil.
3. Melt the chocolate in a double boiler with the oil. Stir until blended. Remove from heat.
4. Stir in the sugars until dissolved.
5. Using a fork, beat the eggs and the vanilla together.
6. Using a wooden spoon, add to the egg mixture to the chocolate mixture.
7. Gradually add the flour and blend.
8. Add the nuts and chocolate chips and blend.
9. Pour the batter into the prepared pan. Bake for 20-25 minutes at 350 degrees F. Top will look dry and feel firm to the touch.
10. Cool on a wire rack before glazing.

GLAZE

1. Melt the chocolate in a double boiler with the oil, corn syrup and coffee granules. Stir until smooth. Remove from heat and stir in the vanilla. Cool in the refrigerator for 1 hour before spreading over the brownies.
2. Cool the glazed brownies for 1 hour in the refrigerator before cutting into squares and removing from the pan.

Grandpa's Pecan Squares

Ingredients

CRUST

1 ¼ cups unbleached white flour
½ cup confectioner's sugar
½ cup canola oil

TOPPING

½ cup light brown sugar
½ cup granulated sugar
½ cup light corn syrup
3 tablespoons canola oil
¼ teaspoon vanilla extract
1 pinch salt
2 large eggs, at room temperature
1 ½ cups chopped pecans

12-16 SQUARES

Grandpa's Pecan Squares

Directions

CRUST

1. Preheat oven to 350 degrees F.

2. Lightly grease a 9-inch square baking pan with canola oil.

3. Combine the flour and confectioner's sugar. Add the canola oil and blend.

4. Pat the dough over the bottom of the prepared pan, forming a ¼-inch high rim around the sides.

5. Bake for 25-30 minutes at 350 degrees F. Allow the crust to cool in pan for 15 minutes before adding the topping.

TOPPING

1. Blend both sugars, the corn syrup, oil, vanilla and salt together with an electric mixer on medium-low speed.

2. Add the eggs, one at a time, on medium speed until blended.

3. Using a wooden spoon, fold in the nuts.

4. Pour the batter over the cooled crust. Bake for 50-55 minutes at 325 degrees F. The top will be dark golden brown.

5. Cool on a wire rack for 15 minutes. Loosen the edges with a sharp knife. Cool completely before cutting into squares and removing from the pan.

Lemon Squares

Ingredients

CRUST

1 cup unbleached white flour
½ cup confectioner's sugar
¼ teaspoon baking soda
1 pinch salt
½ cup canola oil

TOPPING

2 large eggs, at room temperature
1 cup granulated sugar
2 tablespoons unbleached white flour
½ teaspoon baking soda
1½ tablespoons grated lemon zest
3 tablespoons fresh lemon juice
3 tablespoons confectioner's sugar *(for sprinkling)*

12-16 SQUARES

Lemon Squares

Directions

~~~

CRUST

1. Preheat oven to 350 degrees F.
2. Lightly grease a 9-inch square baking pan with canola oil.
3. Combine the flour, sugar, baking soda and salt. Add the canola oil and blend.
4. Press the dough into the prepared pan and bake at 350 degrees F. for 12-15 minutes or until lightly golden.
5. Cool on a wire rack for 15 minutes before adding the topping.

TOPPING

1. Using an electric mixer on high speed, whisk the eggs together until frothed.
2. Add the remaining ingredients (except the confectioner's sugar) on medium speed until blended.
3. Pour the topping over the cooled crust and bake at 350 degrees F. for 15 minutes. The top will set and be lightly golden.
4. Cool completely on a wire rack before sprinkling with the confectioner's sugar.
5. Cut into squares and remove from the pan.

Mahealani's Da' Kine Key Lime Squares

Ingredients

CRUST

1 cup unbleached white flour
½ cup confectioner's sugar
¼ teaspoon baking soda
1 pinch salt
½ cup canola oil

TOPPING

2 large eggs, at room temperature
1 cup granulated sugar
2 tablespoons unbleached white flour
1½ tablespoons grated lime zest
¼ cup lime juice *(about 2-3 limes)*
¼ cup shredded coconut, toasted

12-16 SQUARES

Mahealani's Da' Kine
Key Lime Squares

Directions

~⟳

CRUST

1. Preheat oven to 350 degrees F.

2. Lightly grease a 9-inch square baking pan with canola oil.

3. Combine the flour, sugar, baking soda and salt. Add the canola oil and blend.

4. Press the dough into the prepared pan and bake at 350 degrees F. for 8-10 minutes or until lightly golden.

5. Cool on a wire rack for 15 minutes before adding the topping.

TOPPING

1. Whisk the eggs, sugar and flour together in a medium sized bowl until smooth.

2. Whisk in the lime zest and lime juice and flour until blended.

3. Pour the topping over the cooled crust and bake at 350 degrees F. for 15 minutes. The top will set and be lightly golden

4. Cool completely on a wire rack before sprinkling with the coconut.

5. Cut into squares and remove from the pan.

Raspberry Squares

Ingredients

CRUST

¾ cup canola oil
2 cups confectioner's sugar
1 teaspoon ground cinnamon
1 grated rind of a small lemon
2 large eggs, at room temperature
1½ cups unbleached white flour
1 cup finely chopped cashews

FILLING

¾ cup raspberry preserves

TOPPING

3 tablespoons chopped cashews

12-16 SQUARES

Raspberry Squares
Directions

1. Blend the oil, sugar, cinnamon and lemon zest with an electric mixer on medium-low speed.
2. Add eggs, one at a time, until blended.
3. Gradually add the flour and cashews on low speed until blended.
4. Divide the dough in two and wrap each half in plastic wrap. Refrigerate for a minimum of 4 hours.
5. 20 minutes before baking, preheat oven to 350 degrees F.
6. Lightly grease 9-inch square pan with canola oil.
7. Gently press ½ of the chilled dough into the bottom of the prepared pan.
8. Bake for 20-25 minutes at 350 degrees F. Crust will be golden brown but not hard.
9. Refrigerate for 20 minutes after baking.
10. While the crust is baking, roll out the 2nd half of the dough into a 10-inch square.
11. When the crust is cool, spread the raspberry preserves evenly over it, leaving about a ¼-inch border on all 4 sides.
12. Place the rolled out dough over the preserves and press down around the edges.
13. Lightly brush the crust with canola oil and sprinkle the chopped cashews over the top.
14. Bake for 40-45 minutes at 350 degrees F. The top will be golden brown.
15. Allow the squares to cool for 15 minutes before loosening the sides with a knife. Allow the squares to cool completely before cutting.

Triple Decker Brownies

Ingredients

BOTTOM LAYER

½ cup unbleached white flour

¼ teaspoon baking soda

1 pinch salt

¾ cup quick cooking oats

½ cup light brown sugar *(lightly packed)*

⅓ cup canola oil

MIDDLE LAYER

1 ounce semisweet chocolate

¼ cup canola oil

⅔ cup unbleached white flour

¼ teaspoon baking powder

1 pinch salt

¾ cup granulated sugar

¼ cup cold black coffee

1 large egg, at room temperature

½ teaspoon vanilla

½ cup chopped cashews

TOP LAYER

1 ounce unsweetened chocolate

2 tablespoons canola oil

1½ cups confectioner's sugar

1 teaspoon vanilla

2 tablespoons boiling water

Important: Read the ingredients list on chocolate chips and bars for baking. Do not use any with butter, whey, lactose or any other dairy product.

24-36 SQUARES

Triple Decker Brownies
Directions

BOTTOM LAYER

1. Preheat oven to 350 degrees F.

2. Lightly grease an 11x9x2-inch baking pan with canola oil

3. Combine the flour, baking soda, salt, oats and brown sugar. Stir in the canola oil until blended.

4. Pat the mixture into the prepared pan and bake for 10 minutes at 350 degrees F.

MIDDLE LAYER

1. Melt the chocolate in a double boiler with the oil. Stir until blended. Remove from heat.

2. Combine the flour, baking powder and salt together. Set aside.

3. Blend the sugar and coffee together with an electric mixer on medium speed.

4. Add the egg, then the vanilla and then the chocolate mixture on low speed until blended.

5. Gradually add flour mixture until blended.

6. Using a spatula, fold in the nuts.

7. Pour over the bottom layer and bake for 25 minutes at 350 degrees F. Cool completely.

TOP LAYER

1. Melt the chocolate in a double boiler with the oil. Stir until blended. Remove from heat.

2. Add confectioner's sugar and vanilla. Blend in enough boiling water to make an almost pourable consistency. Spread over cooled brownies. Cool for 1 hour before cutting into squares.

II
Cakes
&
Tortes

Angel Cake

Ingredients

1 cup unbleached white flour
1½ cups granulated sugar
12 large egg whites, at room temperature
1¼ teaspoons cream of tartar
1 pinch salt
1 teaspoon vanilla extract
½ teaspoon almond extract

12-16 SERVINGS

Angel Cake

Directions

1. Preheat oven to 325 degrees F.
2. Set aside an ungreased 10-inch tube pan with removable bottom.
3. Combine the flour and ¾ cup sugar. Set aside.
4. Beat the egg whites with an electric mixer on high speed until frothed. Add the cream of tartar and salt and continue beating until the egg whites form soft peaks.
5. Gradually add the remaining ¾ cup sugar on medium speed until blended.
6. Add the vanilla and almond extract on medium speed until blended.
7. Sift about ¼ cup of the flour mixture over the meringue and using a spatula, fold in until no flour shows.
8. Repeat the process until all of the flour mixture has been blended.
9. Pour the batter into the tube pan. Bake for 1 hour at 325 degrees F. Cake will pull away from the sides of the pan and be golden brown.
10. Invert the pan on to a wire rack. Cool completely before removing from the pan.

Applesauce-Raisin Spice Cake

Ingredients

CAKE

2 cups unbleached white flour

1½ teaspoons baking soda

1 pinch salt

½ cup canola oil

1 cup granulated sugar

½ cup light brown sugar *(firmly packed)*

1½ teaspoons ground cinnamon

1½ teaspoons ground nutmeg

1 teaspoon ground cloves

½ teaspoon ground ginger

½ teaspoon ground allspice

3 tablespoons unsweetened cocoa powder

2 large eggs, at room temperature

1½ cups applesauce

1 cup chopped walnuts

1 cup raisins

GLAZE

1½ cups confectioner's sugar

2 teaspoons ground ginger

1 teaspoon ground cinnamon

1 teaspoon ground allspice

3 tablespoons orange juice

⅓ cup boiling water

12-16 SERVINGS

Applesauce-Raisin Spice Cake

Directions

CAKE

1. Preheat oven to 350 degrees F.
2. Generously grease (with canola oil) and flour a 10-inch bundt pan.
3. Combine flour, baking soda and salt. Set aside.
4. Blend the oil, both sugars, all the spices and the cocoa together with an electric mixer on medium-high speed.
5. Add eggs, one at a time, on medium speed until blended.
6. Add the applesauce on medium speed until blended.
7. Gradually add the flour mixture on low speed until completely blended.
8. Using a wooden spoon, fold in nuts and raisins.
9. Pour the batter into the prepared pan. Bake for 1 hour and 10 minutes at 350 degrees F. The cake will pull away from the sides of the pan.
10. Cool completely on a wire rack before removing from the pan.

GLAZE

1. Combine the confectioner's sugar and spices.
2. Boil water and measure out ⅓ cup.
3. Using a fork combine the orange juice with the sugar mixture. Add just enough boiling water to make a soft spreadable icing.
4. Pour over the cooled cake, allowing it to run down the sides. Allow glaze to set before serving.

Bavarian Marble Gugelhopf

Ingredients

⅓ cup semisweet chocolate chips

2 cups unbleached white flour

3 teaspoons baking powder

1 pinch salt

⅔ cup canola oil

1 cup granulated sugar

4 large eggs, at room temperature

1 teaspoon vanilla extract

½ cup orange juice

2 tablespoons confectioner's sugar *(for sprinkling)*

Important: Be sure to read the ingredients list on semisweet chocolate chips and semisweet solid bars for baking. Do not use brands that have butter fat, anhydrous butter, whey, lactose or any other dairy product.

16 SERVINGS

Bavarian Marble Gugelhopf

Directions

1. Preheat oven to 350 degrees F.
2. Lightly grease a 9-inch fluted tube pan with canola oil.
3. Melt the semisweet chocolate in a double boiler. Allow to cool slightly.
4. Combine flour, baking powder and salt. Set aside.
5. Blend the oil and granulated sugar together with an electric mixer on medium speed.
6. Add eggs, one at a time, until blended.
7. Add the vanilla and orange juice on medium speed until blended.
8. Gradually add flour mixture on low speed.
9. Combine ⅓ of the batter with the chocolate.
10. Pour ⅓ of the plain batter into the tube pan.
11. Pour in ½ of the chocolate batter.
12. Pour in another third of the plain batter.
13. Pour in the 2nd half of the chocolate batter.
14. Pour in the remaining ⅓ of the plain batter.
15. Using a small spatula, cut through the batter in a wide zig-zag. This gives the cake the marbleized effect.
16. Pour into the prepared pan and bake for 50-55 minutes at 350 degrees F. Cake will pull away from the sides of the pan.
17. Cool on a wire rack for 15 minutes before removing from the pan.
18. Sprinkle cake with confectioner's sugar.

Black Magic Chocolate Cake

Ingredients

CAKE

2 cups unbleached white flour

2 teaspoons baking powder

2 teaspoons baking soda

1 pinch salt

¾ cup powdered cocoa

¼ cup canola oil

2½ cups granulated sugar

2 teaspoons vanilla

2 large eggs, at room temperature

1 cup cold black coffee

1 cup orange juice

FROSTING

1 Chocolate Frosting recipe *(pages 218-219)*

24 SQUARES

Black Magic Chocolate Cake

Directions

CAKE

1. Preheat oven to 350 degrees F.
2. Lightly grease (with canola oil) and flour an 11x9x2-inch baking pan.
3. Combine the flour, baking powder, baking soda, salt and cocoa. Set aside.
4. Blend the oil, sugar and vanilla together with an electric mixer on medium speed until smooth.
5. Add eggs, one at a time, on medium speed until blended.
6. Add the coffee and orange juice on medium speed until blended.
7. Gradually add the flour mixture on low speed until blended.
8. Pour the batter into the prepared pan. Bake for 30-35 minutes at 350 degrees F. Cake will pull away from the sides.
9. Cool completely in the pan before frosting.

FROSTING

1. Using a spatula, spread the frosting evenly over the cooled cake and cut into squares.

Boston Cream Pie

Ingredients

CUSTARD

3 tablespoons cornstarch

1 cup water

2 large eggs, at room temperature

¾ cup granulated sugar

1 pinch salt

1 tablespoon vanilla extract

CAKE

1 Yellow Cake recipe *(pages 84-85)*

ICING

1 Chocolate Icing recipe *(pages 220-221)*

10-12 SERVINGS

Boston Cream Pie

Directions

CUSTARD

1. Dissolve the cornstarch in ½ cup water.
2. Add the eggs and whisk until blended.
3. Combine the ½ cup water, sugar and salt in a small sauce pan and heat until the sugar dissolves.
4. Add the cornstarch mixture to the hot liquid, stirring constantly.
5. Add vanilla, stirring constantly for 3-4 minutes. Mixture will thicken. Cook for 1 minute more.
6. Remove custard from heat and pour into a bowl.
7. Allow custard to cool in the bowl for 15 minutes before covering with plastic wrap.
8. Refrigerate for 1 hour before using.

CAKE

1. Bake the Yellow Cake according to the directions on pages 84-85.

ICING

1. Prepare the Chocolate Icing according to the directions on pages 220-221.

ASSEMBLY

1. Spread custard evenly over the bottom cake layer. Place the second cake on top of the custard.
2. Pour prepared icing over the top of the cake. Let some of it run down the sides. Refrigerate for 1 hour before serving.

Carrot-Raisin Cake

Ingredients

CAKE

2 cups unbleached white flour

2 teaspoons baking powder

2 teaspoons baking soda

2 teaspoons cinnamon

1 pinch salt

1½ cups canola oil

2 cups granulated sugar

2 teaspoons vanilla extract

4 large eggs, at room temperature

6 cups *(about 3 pounds)* carrots, peeled and coarsely shredded

½ cup raisins

½ cup chopped cashews

ICING

1 White Icing recipe *(pages 232-233)*

12 SERVINGS

Carrot-Raisin Cake

Directions

~◦~

CAKE

1. Preheat oven to 350 degrees F.
2. Line the bottom of 2 9-inch layer cake pans with wax paper cut to fit the bottom of the pans. Lightly grease with canola oil. Flour the bottom.
3. Combine the flour, baking powder, baking soda, cinnamon and salt. Set aside.
4. Blend the oil, sugar and vanilla together with an electric mixer on medium speed.
5. Add the eggs, one at a time, on medium speed until blended.
6. Gradually add the flour mixture on low speed until blended.
7. Using a spatula, fold in the carrots, raisins and nuts.
8. Pour the batter into the prepared pans. Bake for 35-40 minutes at 350 degrees F. Cake top will spring back when gently pressed.
9. Cool on a wire rack for 10 minutes before removing from the pans.
10. Cool completely before frosting.

ICING

1. Using a spatula, spread the frosting evenly over the top and sides of the cooled cake.

Chocolate Chiffon Cake

Ingredients

CAKE

¾ cup boiling water

½ cup unsweetened cocoa

1¾ cups unbleached white flour

1 tablespoon baking powder

1 pinch salt

½ cup canola oil

1¾ cups granulated sugar

7 large eggs, separated, at room temperature

2 teaspoons vanilla extract

½ teaspoon cream of tartar

TOPPING

1 Strawberry Sauce recipe *(pages 228-229)*

OR

½ cup confectioner's sugar

8-10 SERVINGS

Chocolate Chiffon Cake

Directions

1. Preheat oven to 325 degrees F.
2. Set aside an ungreased 10-inch tube pan.
3. Combine boiling water and cocoa in a small bowl and stir until dissolved. Set aside.
4. Combine the flour, baking powder and salt. Set aside.
5. Blend the oil and granulated sugar together with an electric mixer on medium speed.
6. Add egg yolks and vanilla on medium speed.
7. Add cocoa mixture and blend on low speed.
8. Gradually add the flour mixture on low speed. Set the batter aside.
9. Beat the egg whites with an electric mixture on high speed until frothed. Add the cream of tartar and continue beating until the egg whites form soft peaks.
10. Using a spatula, mix ¼ of the egg whites into the batter and blend. Gently fold in the remaining egg whites. Do not deflate the batter by stirring too much.
11. Pour the batter into the tube pan. Bake for 50 minutes at 325 degrees F. Increase the temperature to 350 degrees F. and bake for 10 minutes more. Cake will pull away from the sides of the pan.
12. Invert the pan on to a wire rack. Cool completely before removing from the pan.
13. Sprinkle with confectioner's sugar or serve with Strawberry Sauce.

Chocolate Decadence

Ingredients

CAKE

16 ounces semisweet chocolate

½ cup canola oil

4 large eggs, at room temperature

1 tablespoon granulated sugar

1 tablespoon unbleached white flour

TOPPING

½ cup fresh raspberries

1 Raspberry Sauce recipe *(pages 226-227)*

¼ cup confectioner's sugar *(for sprinkling)*

OR

6 large strawberries cut into halves with stems attached

1 Strawberry Sauce recipe *(pages 228-229)*

¼ cup confectioner's sugar *(for sprinkling)*

10-12 SERVINGS

Chocolate Decadence

Directions

CAKE

1. Preheat oven to 425 degrees F.
2. Line the bottom of an 8-inch spring form pan with wax paper cut to fit the bottom of the pan. Lightly grease with canola oil. Flour the bottom.
3. Melt the chocolate and oil in a double boiler. Stir until blended. Remove from heat and let stand for 5 minutes.
4. Blend the eggs and sugar together with an electric mixer on medium speed until smooth and the mixture has tripled in volume.
5. Add flour on low speed until blended.
6. Using a spatula, stir in ⅓ of the egg mixture into the chocolate mixture.
7. Gently fold in the remaining egg mixture.
8. Pour the batter into the prepared pan. Bake for EXACTLY 15 minutes at 425 degrees F.
9. Cool completely on a wire rack before removing from the pan. Remove wax paper.

TOPPING

1. Sprinkle the cooled cake with confectioner's sugar. Decorate with the fresh fruit.
2. Cut into small wedges and serve on the raspberry sauce.

Chocolate Layer Cake

Ingredients

CAKE

2 cups unbleached white flour

2 teaspoons baking powder

½ teaspoon baking soda

½ cup cocoa

1 pinch salt

½ cup canola oil

1½ cups granulated sugar

1 cup warm water

½ teaspoon vanilla extract

2 large eggs, at room temperature

FROSTING

1 Chocolate Frosting recipe *(pages 218-219)*

12 SERVINGS

Chocolate Layer Cake

Directions

⌁

CAKE

1. Preheat oven to 350 degrees F.
2. Line the bottom of 2 9-inch layer cake pans with wax paper cut to fit the bottom of the pans. Lightly grease with canola oil. Flour the bottom.
3. Combine the flour, baking powder, baking soda, cocoa and salt. Set aside.
4. Blend the oil, sugar, water and vanilla together with an electric mixer on medium speed.
5. Add eggs, one at a time, on medium speed until blended.
6. Gradually add the flour mixture on low speed until blended.
7. Pour the batter into the prepared pans. Bake for 20 minutes at 350 degrees F. Cake will pull away from the sides and top will spring back when touched.
8. Cool on a wire rack for 10 minutes before removing from pan.
9. Cool completely before frosting.

FROSTING

1. Using a spatula, spread the frosting evenly over the top and sides of the cake.

Chocolate Pudding Cake

Ingredients

CAKE

2 ounces unsweetened chocolate
1 cup unbleached white flour
1½ teaspoons baking powder
1 pinch salt
½ cup canola oil
¾ cup granulated sugar
1 teaspoon vanilla extract
½ cup orange juice

TOPPING

¾ cup granulated sugar
½ cup dark brown sugar *(firmly packed)*
3 tablespoons *(heaping)* unsweetened cocoa
1½ cups boiling water
1 teaspoon vanilla extract

8 SERVINGS

Chocolate Pudding Cake

Directions

CAKE

1. Preheat oven to 350 degrees F.
2. Lightly grease a 9-inch square baking pan with canola oil.
3. Melt the chocolate in a double boiler. Remove from heat.
4. Combine the flour, baking powder and salt. Set aside.
5. Blend the oil, sugar and vanilla together with an electric mixer on medium speed.
6. Add orange juice and mix on low speed until blended.
7. Gradually add flour mixture on low speed until blended.
8. Using a spatula, fold in the chocolate until blended.
9. Pour the batter into the prepared pan.

TOPPING

1. Combine the granulated sugar, brown sugar and cocoa together and blend with a fork.
2. Sprinkle the cocoa mixture over the batter.
3. Combine the boiling water and vanilla.
4. Gently pour the water mixture over the topping without disturbing the topping.
5. Bake for 1 hour at 350 degrees F. The top will be firm.
6. Cool slightly before serving.

Cinnamon Coffee Cake

Ingredients

SWIRL

¼ cup light brown sugar *(firmly packed)*

⅓ cup granulated sugar

2 tablespoons ground cinnamon

1 pinch salt

3 tablespoons light corn syrup

2 tablespoons canola oil

BATTER

2½ cups unbleached white flour

1 tablespoon baking powder

1 pinch salt

2 tablespoons canola oil

1 cup granulated sugar

1 cup orange juice

1 tablespoon vanilla

1 large egg, at room temperature

2 large egg whites, at room temperature

12 SERVINGS

Cinnamon Coffee Cake

Directions

SWIRL

1. Combine sugars, cinnamon and salt. Stir in the corn syrup and oil until blended. Set aside.

BATTER

1. Preheat oven to 350 degrees F.
2. Lightly grease (with canola oil) and flour a 9-inch fluted tube pan.
3. Combine the flour, baking powder and salt. Set aside.
4. Blend the oil, sugar, orange juice and vanilla together with an electric mixer on medium speed.
5. Add the egg and egg whites, one at a time, on medium speed until blended.
6. Gradually add the flour mixture on low speed until blended.
7. Pour the batter into the prepared pan. Sprinkle the cinnamon mixture on top.
8. Using a small spatula, cut through the batter in a wide zig-zag. This gives the cake the swirl effect.
9. Bake for 30-35 minutes at 350 degrees F. Cake will pull away from the sides of the pan.
10. Cool completely on a wire rack before removing from the pan.

Devil's Food Cake

Ingredients

CAKE

3 ounces unsweetened chocolate

2¼ cups unbleached white flour

2 teaspoons baking soda

1 pinch salt

1 cup canola oil

2¼ cups dark brown sugar *(firmly packed)*

3 large eggs, at room temperature

½ cup orange juice

1 cup boiling water

1 teaspoon vanilla extract

FILLING

1 Raspberry Sauce recipe *(pages 226-227)*

FROSTING

1 Chocolate Frosting recipe *(pages 218-219)*

12 SERVINGS

Devil's Food Cake

Directions

CAKE

1. Preheat oven to 375 degrees F.
2. Line the bottom of 2 9-inch layer cake pans with wax paper cut to fit the bottom of the pans. Lightly grease with canola oil. Flour the bottom.
3. Melt the chocolate in a double boiler. Set aside.
4. Combine the flour, baking soda and salt. Set aside.
5. Blend the oil and sugar together with an electric mixer on medium speed until combined.
6. Add the eggs, one at a time, on medium speed.
7. Add the melted chocolate on medium speed.
8. Alternately add the flour mixture and the orange juice on low speed until blended
9. Add the boiling water and vanilla on low speed until blended.
10. Pour the batter into the prepared pans. Bake for 25-30 minutes at 375 degrees F. Top will spring back when touched.
11. Cool on a wire rack for 10 minutes before removing from pan. Cool completely on a wire rack before assembling.

FILLING

1. Using a spatula, spread the raspberry sauce evenly between the layers of the cake.

ICING

1. Using a spatula, spread the icing evenly over the top and sides of the cake.

Easter Cake

Ingredients

CAKE

2½ cups unbleached white flour

2 teaspoons baking powder

1 pinch salt

1 cup canola oil

1 cup granulated sugar

3 large eggs, at room temperature

8 ounces of almond paste

¼ cup orange juice

FILLING

1 Almond Custard Recipe *(pages 216-217)*

FROSTING

6 ounces semisweet chocolate

2 tablespoons orange juice

2 tablespoons canola oil

8-12 SERVINGS

Easter Cake

Directions

CUSTARD

1. Prepare custard according to directions.

CAKE

1. Preheat oven to 350 degrees F.
2. Lightly grease (with canola oil) and flour a 9-inch fluted tube pan.
3. Combine the flour, baking powder and salt. Set aside.
4. Blend the oil and sugar together with an electric mixer on medium speed.
5. Add the eggs, one at a time, on medium speed until blended.
6. Cut the almond paste into small pieces and gradually add to the batter on high speed. The batter will be lumpy.
7. Add the orange juice on low speed until blended.
8. Gradually add the flour mixture on low speed until blended.
9. Pour the batter into the prepared pan. Bake for 45 minutes at 350 degrees F. Cake will pull away from the sides and be golden brown.
10. Cool completely before cutting into three layers.
11. Using a spatula, spread the almond custard between the layers. Reassemble the cake.

FROSTING

1. Melt the chocolate in a double boiler with the orange juice and oil. Stir until blended. Cool slightly and pour over assembled cake.

Elise's Friendship Cake

Ingredients

6 large apples, peeled, cored and thinly sliced
½ cup granulated sugar
1 teaspoon cinnamon
½ cup chopped cashews
1 cup unbleached white flour
¾ cup granulated sugar
¾ teaspoon baking powder
1 pinch salt
1 large egg, at room temperature
½ cup orange juice
½ cup canola oil or apple sauce

8 SERVINGS

Elise's Friendship Cake

Directions

1. Preheat oven to 325 degrees F.
2. Lightly grease a 9-inch pie plate with canola oil.
3. Place the prepared apples into the prepared baking dish.
4. Sprinkle ½ cup sugar and the cinnamon over the apples.
5. Sprinkle the chopped cashews over the apples.
6. Combine the flour, ¾ cup sugar, baking powder and salt. Set aside.
7. Combine the egg, orange juice and oil and blend with a fork.
8. Add the egg mixture all at once to the flour mixture and blend until smooth.
9. Pour the batter over the apples. Bake for 55-60 minutes at 325 degrees F. Top will be golden brown. Serve warm.

Koenigskuchen

Ingredients

4 cups unbleached white flour
4 teaspoons baking powder
1 pinch salt
1¼ cups canola oil
1 cup granulated sugar
⅔ cup white wine
1 teaspoon vanilla extract
1 teaspoon lemon juice
4 large eggs, at room temperature
1½ cups currants
⅔ cup raisins
⅓ cup lemon zest

12 SERVINGS

Koenigskuchen

Directions

1. Preheat oven to 325 degrees F.
2. Line the bottom of a 4x8-inch loaf pan with wax paper cut to fit the bottom of the pan. Lightly grease with canola oil. Flour the bottom.
3. Combine the flour, baking powder and salt. Set aside.
4. Blend the oil, sugar, wine, vanilla and lemon juice together with an electric mixer on medium speed.
5. Add eggs, one at a time, on medium speed until blended.
6. Gradually add the flour mixture on low speed until blended.
7. Using a spatula, fold in the currants, raisins and lemon zest.
8. Pour the batter into the prepared pan. Bake for 1 hour and 15 minutes at 325 degrees F. Cake will pull away from the sides and the top will spring back when touched.
9. Cool on a wire rack for 10 minutes before removing from the pan.

Maine Blueberry Crumb Cake

Ingredients

TOPPING

½ cup unbleached white flour
½ cup granulated sugar
½ cup light brown sugar
¼ teaspoon ground cinnamon
1 pinch salt
¼ cup canola oil

CAKE

2 cups unbleached white flour
2 teaspoons baking powder
1 pinch salt
¼ cup canola oil
1½ cup sugar
1½ teaspoons vanilla extract
2 large eggs, at room temperature
¾ cup orange juice
2 cups Maine blueberries

12 SERVINGS

Maine Blueberry Crumb Cake

Directions

TOPPING

1. Combine all of the ingredients together.
2. Add the oil and toss with a fork until coarse crumbs form. Set aside.

CAKE

1. Preheat oven to 350 degrees F.
2. Lightly grease a 9-inch square baking pan with canola oil.
3. Combine the flour, baking powder and salt. Set aside.
4. Blend the oil, sugar and vanilla together with an electric mixer on medium speed.
5. Add the eggs, one at a time, on medium speed until blended.
6. Alternately add the flour mixture and the orange juice on low speed until blended.
7. Using a spatula, gently fold in the blueberries.
8. Pour the batter into the prepared pan. Bake for 1 hour at 350 degrees F. *Cake top should set but NOT be golden brown.*
9. When the top of the cake has set, spread the topping onto the cake and bake for 20 minutes more.
10. Remove the cake from the oven and serve hot.

Mocha Jake's Cake

Ingredients

CAKE

2 cups unbleached white flour

¾ cup unsweetened cocoa

2 teaspoons baking powder

1 teaspoon baking soda

1 teaspoon cinnamon

1 pinch salt

¾ cup canola oil

1½ cups granulated sugar

1 teaspoon vanilla extract

3 large eggs, at room temperature

1 tablespoon instant coffee granules

1¼ cups boiling water

TOPPING

1 Mocha Jake Sauce recipe *(pages 224-225)*

12-14 SERVINGS

Mocha Jake's Cake

Directions

CAKE

1. Preheat oven to 350 degrees F.
2. Line the bottom of a 9-inch spring form pan with wax paper cut to fit the bottom of the pan. Lightly grease with canola oil. Flour the bottom.
3. Combine the flour, cocoa, baking powder, baking soda, cinnamon and salt. Set aside.
4. Blend the oil, sugar and vanilla together with an electric mixer on medium speed.
5. Add the eggs, one at a time, on medium speed until blended.
6. Add the coffee granules to the boiling water.
7. Alternately add the flour mixture and coffee on low speed until blended.
8. Pour the batter into the prepared pan. Bake for 50-55 minutes at 350 degrees F. Cake will pull away from the sides.
9. Cool on a wire rack for 10 minutes before removing from the pan. Peel the wax paper from the bottom of the cake and cool completely on a wire rack before adding the sauce.

TOPPING

1. Using a spatula, spread the sauce evenly over the top of the cake. Reserve any excess and serve with the cake.

Orange Chiffon Cake
with Lemon Glaze

Ingredients

CAKE

1¼ cups unbleached white flour
1 tablespoon baking powder
1 pinch salt
1½ cups granulated sugar
½ cup canola oil
¾ cup orange juice
1 tablespoon orange zest
6 large eggs, separated, at room temperature
½ cup granulated sugar

GLAZE

¼ cup canola oil
2 cups confectioner's sugar
½ cup boiling water
½ cup lemon juice *(approximately 2 lemons)*

OPTIONAL

2 cups fresh strawberries

12-16 SERVINGS

Orange Chiffon Cake
with Lemon Glaze

Directions

➤━━○

CAKE

1. Preheat oven to 325 degrees F.

2. Set aside an ungreased 10-inch tube pan with a removable bottom.

3. Combine the flour, baking powder, salt and 1½ cup sugar. Set aside.

4. Blend the oil, orange juice, orange zest and egg yolk together with an electric mixer on medium speed.

5. Gradually add the flour mixture to the egg mixture with an electric mixer on low speed until blended. Set aside.

6. Beat the egg whites on medium-high speed until frothed. Gradually add ½ cup sugar and continue beating until the egg whites form stiff peaks (about 1 minute). Stir ⅓ of the egg whites into the batter. Using a spatula, fold in the remaining egg whites.

7. Pour the batter into the tube pan. Bake 1 hour at 325 degrees F. Cake will be golden brown.

GLAZE

1. Blend the oil, confectioner's sugar and water together. Add the lemon juice and blend.

2. When the cake has completely cooled, remove from the pan. Pour half of the glaze over the cake. Let stand 30 minutes. Pour the remaining glaze over the cake before serving. Best eaten the day the cake is baked.

Orange-Raisin Cake
with Lemon Glaze

Ingredients

CAKE

3 cups unbleached white flour

1½ teaspoons baking powder

1½ teaspoons baking soda

1 pinch salt

1½ oranges with rind, cut into chunks with seeds
   removed

1½ cups raisins

1 cup cashews, coarsely chopped

¾ cup canola oil

1½ cups granulated sugar

1 tablespoon grated lemon zest

3 large eggs, at room temperature

1½ cups orange juice

GLAZE

½ cup lemon juice

¼ cup orange juice

5 tablespoons granulated sugar

12-16 SERVINGS

Orange-Raisin Cake
with Lemon Glaze

Directions

⤙⤚

CAKE

1. Preheat oven to 350 degrees F.

2. Lightly grease a 10-inch bundt pan with canola oil.

3. Combine the flour, baking powder, baking soda and salt. Set aside.

4. Put oranges and raisins into a food processor and process until coarsely chopped. Add chopped nuts. Set aside.

5. Blend the oil, sugar and lemon zest together with an electric mixer on medium speed.

6. Add eggs, one at a time, on medium speed until blended.

7. Add the orange mixture on low speed until blended. Batter will appear curdled.

8. Alternately add the flour mixture and the orange juice on low speed. Do not completely blend with each addition.

9. Pour the batter into the prepared pan. Bake 1¼ hours at 350 degrees F. Cool completely on a wire rack before removing from pan.

GLAZE

1. Prepare the glaze by blending all the ingredients together.

2. When cake has cooled, remove it from the pan, place on serving plate, poke holes over the entire cake with a fork. Baste the cake with the lemon glaze.

Pineapple-Carrot Spice Cake

Ingredients

2 cups unbleached white flour

2 teaspoons baking powder

1½ teaspoons baking soda

1 pinch salt

2 teaspoons ground cinnamon

½ teaspoons ground cloves

½ teaspoons allspice

½ teaspoons ground mace

1 cup crushed pineapple, drained

2 cups grated carrots *(about 4 carrots)*

½ cup chopped walnuts

1½ cups granulated sugar

1½ cups canola oil

1 teaspoon vanilla extract

4 large eggs, at room temperature

12-16 SERVINGS

Pineapple-Carrot Spice Cake

Directions

1. Preheat oven to 350 degrees F.
2. Lightly grease (with canola oil) and flour a 10-inch bundt pan.
3. Combine the flour, baking powder, baking soda, salt, cinnamon, ground cloves, allspice, and ground mace. Set aside.
4. Combine the pineapple, grated carrots and nuts and mix together. Set aside.
5. Blend the sugar, oil and vanilla together with an electric mixer on medium speed.
6. Add eggs, one at a time, on medium speed until blended.
7. Gradually add the flour mixture on low speed until completely blended.
8. Using a wooden spoon, blend in the pineapple mixture.
9. Pour the batter into the prepared pan and bake for 45 minutes at 350 degrees F. Turn the oven down to 300 degrees F. and bake for 10 minutes more.
10. Cool on a wire rack for 10 minutes before removing from the pan. Cool completely before serving.

"Side Cake"

AKA

Pineapple Upside-Down Cake

Ingredients

4 tablespoons canola oil

¾ cup light brown sugar *(lightly packed)*

9 slices canned pineapple, drained, with juices set aside

1½ cups unbleached white flour

1½ teaspoons baking powder

1 pinch salt

½ cup canola oil

½ cup granulated sugar

½ teaspoon vanilla extract

1 large egg, at room temperature

½ cup pineapple juice

6 SERVINGS

"Side Cake"

AKA

Pineapple Upside-Down Cake

Directions

1. Preheat oven to 375 degrees F.
2. Pour the 4 tablespoons of canola oil into a 9-inch square baking pan and sprinkle with the brown sugar.
3. Arrange the pineapple slices in a pattern on top of the sugar. *(Be creative!)*
4. Combine the flour, baking powder and salt. Set aside.
5. Blend the ½ cup oil, granulated sugar and vanilla together with an electric mixer on medium speed.
6. Add the egg on medium speed until blended.
7. Add the pineapple juice on low speed until blended.
8. Gradually add the flour mixture on low speed until blended.
9. Spoon the batter over the pineapple slices. Bake for 35-40 minutes at 375 degrees F.
10. Cool on a wire rack for 5 minutes before inverting the cake onto a serving platter and removing the pan. The pineapple will be on top.

Red Wine Cake

Ingredients

CAKE

4 ounces semisweet chocolate

2 cups unbleached white flour

1 teaspoon baking powder

1 teaspoon cocoa powder

1 pinch salt

1 cup canola oil

1 cup granulated sugar

1½ teaspoons vanilla extract

4 large eggs, at room temperature

½ cup red wine

3 tablespoons confectioner's sugar *(for sprinkling)*

SAUCE

1 Raspberry Sauce Recipe *(pages 226-227)*

Important: Be sure to read the ingredients list on semisweet chocolate chips and semisweet solid bars for baking. Do not use brands that have butter fat, anhydrous butter, whey, lactose or any other dairy product.

12 SERVINGS

Red Wine Cake

Directions

1. Preheat oven to 325 degrees F.
2. Lightly grease a 9-inch fluted tube pan with canola oil.
3. Melt the chocolate in a double boiler. Set aside.
4. Combine the flour, baking powder, cocoa powder and salt. Set aside.
5. Blend the oil, sugar and vanilla together with an electric mixer on medium speed.
6. Add the eggs, one at a time, on medium speed until blended.
7. Add the melted chocolate on medium speed until blended.
8. Alternately add the flour mixture and the red wine on low speed until blended.
9. Pour the batter into the prepared pan. Bake for 40-45 minutes at 325 degrees F. Top will spring back when touched.
10. Cool on a wire rack for 10 minutes before removing from the pan.
11. Sprinkle with confectioner's sugar when cool.
12. Serve with Raspberry Sauce.

Regal Chocolate Torte

Ingredients

TORTE

4 ounces semisweet chocolate

4 ounces bittersweet chocolate

¾ cup canola oil

¾ cup granulated sugar

6 large eggs, separated, at room temperature

1½ cups ground cashews

ICING

1 Chocolate Icing recipe *(pages 220-221)*

Important: Be sure to read the ingredients list on semisweet chocolate chips and semisweet solid bars for baking. Do not use brands that have butter fat, anhydrous butter, whey, lactose or any other dairy product.

12 SERVINGS

Regal Chocolate Torte

Directions

TORTE

1. Preheat oven to 350 degrees F.
2. Line the bottom of a 10-inch springform pan with wax paper cut to fit the bottom. Lightly grease with canola oil. Flour the bottom.
3. Melt the chocolates in a double boiler. Allow to cool slightly.
4. Blend the oil and granulated sugar together with an electric mixer on high speed.
5. Add egg yolks, one at a time, until blended.
6. Add the chocolate mixture and nuts on medium speed until blended. Set aside.
7. Beat the egg whites on high speed until stiff peaks form.
8. Using a spatula, gently fold the egg white into the batter. Be careful not to deflate the batter.
9. Pour into the prepared pan. Bake for 50 minutes at 350 degrees F. Cake top will form a light crust. **DO NOT OVER BAKE.**
10. Cool on a wire rack for 15 minutes before removing from the pan.
11. Peel off the wax paper before transferring the torte to a serving platter.

ICING

1. Using a spatula, spread the icing evenly over the top and sides of the cooled cake.

Scandinavian Mocha Cake

Ingredients

2 cups strong hot coffee
2 cups granulated sugar
2 tablespoon cocoa
1 cup seedless raisins, chopped
2 cups unbleached white flour
2 teaspoons baking powder
1 pinch salt
1 teaspoon cinnamon
1 teaspoon ground nutmeg
½ teaspoon ground cloves
½ teaspoon baking soda
½ cup canola oil
½ teaspoon vanilla extract
2 large eggs, at room temperature
¼ cup confectioner's sugar *(for sprinkling)*

12-16 SERVINGS

Scandinavian Mocha Cake

Directions

1. Preheat oven to 350 degrees F.
2. Lightly grease (with canola oil) and flour a 10-inch tube pan.
3. Combine the coffee, 1 cup of granulated sugar, cocoa and raisins in a saucepan. Bring to a boil and simmer for 10-15 minutes. Let cool.
4. Combine the flour, baking powder, salt, cinnamon, nutmeg, cloves and baking soda. Set aside.
5. Blend the oil, remaining 1 cup granulated sugar and vanilla together with an electric mixer on medium speed.
6. Add the eggs, one at a time, on medium speed until blended.
7. Gradually add the flour mixture on low speed until blended.
8. Add the cooled coffee mixture on low speed until blended.
9. Pour the batter into the prepared pan. Bake for 1 hour at 350 degrees F. Cake will pull away from the sides of the pan.
10. Cool on a wire rack for ½ hour before removing from the pan.
11. Sprinkle with confectioner's sugar when cool.

Sponge Cake

Ingredients

1 cup unbleached white flour
1 pinch salt
6 large eggs, at room temperature
1 tablespoon lemon juice
1 teaspoon lemon zest
1 cup granulated sugar

12-16 SERVINGS

Sponge Cake

Directions

1. Preheat oven to 325 degrees F.
2. Lightly grease and flour the bottom (but not the sides) of a 10-inch tube pan.
3. Combine the flour and salt. Set aside.
4. Beat the eggs with an electric mixer on high speed until frothed. Add the lemon juice and lemon zest and continue beating on high until soft peaks form *(about 15 minutes)*.
5. Gradually add the sugar on medium speed until blended.
6. Gradually add the flour mixture on low speed until blended.
7. Pour the batter into the prepared pan. Bake for 45-50 minutes at 325 degrees F. Cake will pull away from the sides and be golden brown.
8. Invert the pan and let the cake cool in the pan on a wire rack to room temperature before removing from the pan.

Stefan's Almond Cake

Ingredients

CAKE

5 cups unbleached white flour

4 teaspoons baking powder

1 pinch salt

2 cups canola oil

2 cups granulated sugar

6 large eggs, at room temperature

16 ounces of almond paste

½ cup orange juice

36 SQUARES

Stefan's Almond Cake

Directions

1. Preheat oven to 350 degrees F.
2. Lightly grease (with canola oil) and flour an 11x9x2-inch baking pan.
3. Combine the flour, baking powder and salt. Set aside.
4. Blend the oil and sugar together with an electric mixer on medium speed.
5. Add the eggs, one at a time, on medium speed until blended.
6. Cut almond paste into small pieces and gradually add to the batter on high speed. The batter will be lumpy.
7. Add the orange juice on low speed until blended.
8. Gradually add the flour mixture on low speed until blended.
9. Pour the batter into the prepared pan. Bake for 50 minutes at 350 degrees F. Cake will pull away from the sides and be golden brown.
10. Cool completely in the pan on a wire rack before cutting into squares and removing from the pan.

Yellow Cake

Ingredients

2½ cups unbleached white flour
2 teaspoons baking powder
½ teaspoon baking soda
1 pinch salt
1 cup canola oil
2 cups granulated sugar
1 cup white wine
1 teaspoon vanilla extract
4 large eggs, at room temperature

12 SERVINGS

Yellow Cake

Directions

1. Preheat oven to 350 degrees F.
2. Line the bottom of 2 9-inch layer cake pans with wax paper cut to fit the bottom of the pans. Lightly grease with canola oil. Flour the bottom.
3. Combine the flour, baking powder, baking soda and salt. Set aside.
4. Blend the oil, sugar, wine and vanilla together with an electric mixer on medium speed.
5. Add the eggs, one at a time, on medium speed until blended.
6. Gradually add the flour mixture on low speed until blended.
7. Pour the batter into the prepared pans. Bake for 25-30 minutes at 350 degrees F. Cake will pull away from the sides and top will spring back when touched.
8. Cool on a wire rack for 10 minutes before removing from the pan.

Zwetschenkuchen
(Plum Cake)

Ingredients

TOPPING

6 Italian plums, washed, depitted and cut into
  connecting quarters.
2 tablespoons granulated sugar
2 tablespoons confectioner's sugar *(for sprinkling)*

PASTRY

1¾ cups unbleached white flour
1 teaspoon baking powder
½ cup canola oil
½ cup granulated sugar
2 teaspoons vanilla extract
1 large egg, at room temperature

16 SERVINGS

Zwetschenkuchen
(Plum Cake)

Directions

TOPPING

1. Prepare plums. Be sure to leave the plum quarters connected when slicing.
2. Sprinkle with granulated sugar. Set aside.

PASTRY

1. Preheat oven to 350 degrees F.
2. Lightly grease a 10-inch spring form pan with canola oil.
3. Combine flour, baking powder. Set aside.
4. Combine the oil, sugar and vanilla together with an electric mixer on medium speed until blended.
5. Add the egg on medium speed until blended.
6. Gradually add the flour mixture on low speed until pastry comes together.
7. Turn pastry on to floured surface and knead until smooth.
8. Roll out the pastry to the size of the prepared pan. Press the pastry ¼ inch up the sides of the pan. Pierce the dough with a fork.
9. Place the plums in a rosette form on the pastry.
10. Bake for 15-20 minutes at 350 degrees F.
11. Sprinkle the cooled cake with confectioner's sugar.

III

Cookies
&
Candies

Grace's Favorite
Chocolate Chip Cookies

Ingredients

2¼ cups unbleached white flour
1 teaspoon baking soda
1 pinch salt
1 cup canola oil
¾ cup light brown sugar *(firmly packed)*
¾ cup granulated sugar
2 large eggs, at room temperature
2 teaspoons vanilla extract
12 ounces semisweet chocolate chips
1 cup chopped cashews *(optional)*

Important: Be sure to read the ingredients list on semisweet chocolate chips and semisweet solid bars for baking. Do not use brands that have butter fat, anhydrous butter, whey, lactose or any other dairy product.

48 COOKIES

Grace's Favorite
Chocolate Chip Cookies

Directions

1. Preheat oven to 375 degrees F.
2. Lightly grease two cookie sheets with canola oil.
3. Combine the flour, baking soda and salt. Set aside.
4. Blend the oil and two sugars together.
5. Blend the eggs and vanilla together with a fork and add to the sugar mixture.
6. Gradually add the flour mixture until blended.
7. Add the chocolate chips and nuts and mix until blended.
8. Drop rounded tablespoon sized mounds of the dough about 1 inch apart onto the prepared cookie sheets.
9. Bake for 9-10 minutes at 375 degrees F.
10. Cool for 1 minute before on the cookie sheet before removing to a wire rack to cool completely.

Chocolate Fudge

Ingredients

1½ cups granulated sugar
2 tablespoons canola oil
1 pinch salt
½ cup orange juice
2 cups semisweet chocolate chips
2 teaspoons vanilla extract
¾ cup coarsely chopped cashews

Important: Be sure to read the ingredients list on semisweet chocolate chips and semisweet solid bars for baking. Do not use brands
that have butter fat, anhydrous butter, whey, lactose or any other
dairy product.

30-36 SQUARES

Chocolate Fudge

Directions

1. Lightly grease an 8-inch square baking pan with canola oil.
2. Combine the sugar, oil, salt and orange juice in a large saucepan over medium heat. Stirring constantly, bring the mixture to a boil. Lower the heat to medium-low and simmer for 5 minutes.
3. Remove the mixture from the heat and stir in the chocolate chips until the chocolate melts.
4. Stir in the vanilla and cashews.
5. Pour into prepared pan, cover and refrigerate for 2 hours. Cut into squares to serve.

Chocolate Macaroons

Ingredients

4 ounces semisweet chocolate
2 ounces unsweetened chocolate
2 large egg whites, at room temperature
½ cup granulated sugar
1 teaspoon vanilla extract
2 cups shredded coconut

Important: Be sure to read the ingredients list on semisweet chocolate chips and semisweet solid bars for baking. Do not use brands that have butter fat, anhydrous butter, whey, lactose or any other dairy product.

12-14 COOKIES

Chocolate Macaroons

Directions

1. Preheat oven to 375 degrees F.
2. Lightly grease a cookie sheet with canola oil.
3. Melt the two chocolates in a double boiler. Stir until blended. Remove from heat and allow to cool slightly.
4. Beat the egg whites with an electric mixer on medium speed until frothy (about ½ a minute). Gradually add the sugar and continue beating until the mixture has the consistency of marshmallow fluff.
5. Blend in the vanilla extract.
6. Using a spatula, gently fold in the melted chocolate.
7. Using a spatula, gently fold in the shredded coconut.
8. Drop tablespoon sized mounds of the dough about 1½ inches apart on to the prepared cookie sheet.
9. Bake for 10-12 minutes at 375 degrees F. or until a light crust forms on the outside of the cookies.
10. Remove the cookies from the cookie sheet very carefully and cool on a wire rack.

Chocolate Moguls

Ingredients

4 large egg whites, at room temperature
1 pinch salt
1¼ cups granulated sugar
1 teaspoon vanilla extract
½ cup semisweet chocolate chips

Important: Be sure to read the ingredients list on semisweet chocolate chips. Do not use brands that have butter fat, anhydrous butter, whey, lactose or any other dairy product.

50 COOKIES

Chocolate Moguls

Directions

1. Preheat oven to 300 degrees F.
2. Lightly grease two cookie sheets with canola oil. Sprinkle flour on the sheets and shake to distribute evenly. Remove excess.
3. Beat the egg whites and salt with an electric mixer on medium-high speed until frothed (about 1 minute). Gradually add the sugar and vanilla on high speed until the egg whites form stiff peaks (about 2 minutes).
4. Using a spatula, gently fold in the chocolate chips.
5. Drop teaspoon sized moguls about 1 inch apart on the prepared cookie sheets.
6. Bake for 20 minutes at 300 degrees F. The moguls will be light brown.
7. Cool completely on the cookie sheets.

Chocolate Raspberry Truffles

Ingredients

8 ounces semisweet chocolate

⅓ cup canola oil

½ cup seedless raspberry jam

3 tablespoons creme de cassis or raspberry flavored
liqueur

⅓ cup confectioner's sugar

Important: Be sure to read the ingredients list on semisweet chocolate chips and semisweet solid bars for baking. Do not use brands that have butter fat, anhydrous butter, whey, lactose or any other dairy product.

32 TRUFFLES

Chocolate Raspberry Truffles

Directions

1. Melt the chocolate in a double boiler with the oil. Remove from heat.
2. Add raspberry jam and liqueur to the chocolate mixture. Stir until blended.
3. Pour into a shallow pan, cover and refrigerate for 3 hours.
4. Pour confectioner's sugar into a shallow bowl.
5. Using a teaspoon, scoop up teaspoon sized pieces of the mixture. Roll the mixture into round balls and roll in the sugar until coated.
6. Place on a serving tray.

Truffles may be stored in the refrigerator for 2 weeks in an airtight container. Remove 30 minutes before serving. Truffles may be frozen up to 4 months in an airtight container. Defrost in the container.

Double Chocolate Chip Cookies

Ingredients

6 ounces semisweet chocolate

½ cup canola oil

3 tablespoons unbleached white flour

2 tablespoons *(heaping)* unsweetened cocoa powder

1 teaspoon baking powder

1 pinch salt

2 large eggs, at room temperature

½ cup granulated sugar

¼ cup light brown sugar *(lightly packed)*

2 teaspoons vanilla extract

12 ounces semisweet chocolate chips

1½ cups coarsely chopped cashews

Important: Be sure to read the ingredients list on semisweet choco-late chips and semisweet solid bars for baking. Do not use brands that have butter fat, anhydrous butter, whey, lactose or any other dairy product.

18-24 COOKIES

Double Chocolate Chip Cookies

Directions

1. Preheat oven to 325 degrees F.
2. Lightly grease two cookie sheets with canola oil.
3. Melt the 6 ounces of semisweet chocolate in a double boiler with the oil. Stir until blended. Set aside.
4. Combine the flour, cocoa powder, baking powder and salt. Set aside.
5. Beat the eggs and both sugars with an electric mixer on high speed until the mixture is light yellow.
6. Add the vanilla and blend.
7. Gradually add the chocolate mixture on medium-low speed until blended.
8. Gradually add the flour mixture on low speed until blended.
9. Using a wooden spoon, stir in the chocolate chips and cashews.
10. Drop heaping tablespoons of the dough about 3 inches apart onto the prepared cookie sheets.
11. Bake for 10-12 minutes at 325 degrees F.
12. Let cool for 2-3 minutes on the cookie sheets before removing to a wire rack to cool completely.

Jaffa Cakes

Ingredients

2 large eggs, at room temperature
½ cup granulated sugar
½ cup unbleached white flour
4 tablespoons marmalade
4 ounces semisweet chocolate
2 tablespoons orange zest *(finely grated)*
2 teaspoons canola oil
1 tablespoon water

Important: Be sure to read the ingredients list on semisweet chocolate chips and semisweet solid bars for baking. Do not use brands that have butter fat, anhydrous butter, whey, lactose or any other dairy product.

18 COOKIES

Jaffa Cakes

Directions

1. Preheat oven to 400 degrees F.
2. Lightly grease 18 muffin cups with canola oil.
3. Blend the eggs and sugar together with an electric mixer on high speed until light yellow.
4. Using a spatula, fold in the flour until blended.
5. Spoon the mixture into the prepared muffin pans.
6. Bake for 8-10 minutes at 400 degrees F. The cookies will be golden brown.
7. Remove immediately from the muffin pans and cool on a wire rack.
8. Spread a little marmalade over each cake.
9. Melt the chocolate in a double boiler with the orange zest, oil and water. Stir until blended. Cool until the chocolate starts to thicken and then spread over each cake.

Oatmeal Cookies

Ingredients

1¾ cups unbleached white flour

1 teaspoon baking soda

1 pinch salt

1 cup canola oil

1¼ cups light brown sugar *(firmly packed)*

½ cup granulated sugar

2 large eggs, at room temperature

2 tablespoons orange juice

2 teaspoons vanilla extract

2½ cups quick cooking oats

1 cup golden raisins **OR** 12 ounces semisweet
chocolate chips

1 cup chopped cashews *(optional)*

Important: Be sure to read the ingredients list on semisweet chocolate chips and semisweet solid bars for baking. Do not use brands that have butter fat, anhydrous butter, whey, lactose or any other dairy product.

60 COOKIES

Oatmeal Cookies

Directions

1. Preheat oven to 375 degrees F.
2. Lightly grease two cookie sheets with canola oil.
3. Combine the flour, baking soda and salt. Set aside.
4. Using a wooden spoon, blend the oil and two sugars together.
5. Blend the eggs, orange juice and vanilla together with a fork and add to the sugar mixture.
6. Gradually add the flour mixture until blended.
7. Add the oats, raisins *(or chocolate chips)* and nuts and mix until blended.
8. Drop rounded tablespoon sized mounds of the dough about 1½ inch apart on the prepared cookie sheets.
9. Bake for 9-10 minutes at 375 degrees F.
10. Cool for 1 minute on the cookie sheets before removing to a wire rack to cool completely.

Peanut Butter & Jelly Cookies

Ingredients

1¾ cups unbleached white flour
½ teaspoon baking soda
⅓ cup canola oil
½ cup light brown sugar *(firmly packed)*
½ cup granulated sugar
1 cup peanut butter
2 large eggs, at room temperature
2 teaspoons vanilla extract
⅓ cup of your favorite jam or jelly
¼ cup granulated sugar

36 COOKIES

Peanut Butter & Jelly Cookies

Directions

1. Preheat oven to 350 degrees F.
2. Lightly grease two cookie sheets with canola oil.
3. Combine the flour and baking soda. Set aside.
4. Blend the oil, brown sugar, ½ cup granulated sugar and peanut butter together with an electric mixture on medium speed until smooth.
5. Add eggs and vanilla and mix on medium speed until blended.
6. Gradually add the flour mixture on low speed until blended.
7. Scoop out 36 large teaspoonfuls of the dough and roll them into balls.
8. Dip one side of each ball into the ¼ cup of granulated sugar and place them sugar side up on the prepared cookie sheet.
9. Indent the center of each cookie and fill the indention with ½ teaspoon of jelly or jam.
10. Bake for 14-16 minutes or until light golden brown. Jam will be melted.
11. Remove the cookies from the cookie sheet very carefully and cool on a wire rack.

Peanut Butter Cookies

Ingredients

1½ cups unbleached white flour
½ teaspoon baking soda
1 pinch salt
½ cup canola oil
½ cup peanut butter
½ cup granulated sugar
½ cup light brown sugar
½ teaspoon vanilla extract
1 large egg, at room temperature

18-20 COOKIES

Peanut Butter Cookies

Directions

1. Combine the flour, baking soda and salt. Set aside.
2. Blend the oil, peanut butter both sugars, and vanilla together with an electric mixer on medium speed.
3. Add the egg and mix on medium speed until blended.
4. Gradually add the flour mixture on low speed until blended.
5. Place the mixture in a covered bowl and refrigerate for 3 hours or overnight.
6. 10 MINUTES BEFORE BAKING, preheat oven to 350 degrees F.
7. Lightly grease two cookie sheets with canola oil.
8. Drop rounded tablespoon sized mounds of the dough about 2 inches apart on to the prepared cookie sheets.
9. Bake for 12-15 minutes at 350 degree F. The cookies will rise slightly and be golden brown on the edges.
10. Cool completely on the cookie sheet before removing.

Raspberry Macaroons

Ingredients

5 large egg whites, at room temperature
1½ cups confectioner's sugar
3 tablespoons seedless red raspberry jam
2 teaspoons vanilla extract
1 cup unbleached white flour
1 *(14 ounce)* bag of shredded coconut

30-36 COOKIES

Raspberry Macaroons

Directions

1. Preheat oven to 350 degrees F.
2. Lightly grease a cookie sheet with canola oil.
3. Beat the egg whites with an electric mixer on medium speed until frothy (about ½ a minute). Gradually add the sugar and continue beating until the mixture has the consistency of marshmallow fluff.
4. Add the raspberry jam and vanilla to the egg mixture on medium speed (the jam will not blend completely).
5. Gradually add the flour on medium-low speed until blended.
6. Using a spatula, gently fold in the coconut.
7. Drop tablespoon sized mounds of the dough about 1½ inches apart on the prepared cookie sheet.
8. Bake for 15-20 minutes at 350 degrees F. or until a light crust forms on the outside of the cookies.
9. Remove the cookies from the cookie sheet very carefully and cool on a wire rack.

Sinfully Chocolate Drops

Ingredients

5 ounces semisweet chocolate

3 ounces unsweetened chocolate

½ cup canola oil

½ cup unbleached white flour

1 teaspoon baking powder

1 pinch salt

2 large eggs, at room temperature

2 teaspoons vanilla extract

1 tablespoon instant coffee granules

¾ cup granulated sugar

¾ cup semisweet chocolate chips

¼ cup chopped pecans

½ cup chopped walnuts

Important: Be sure to read the ingredients list on semisweet chocolate chips and semisweet solid bars for baking. Do not use brands
that have butter fat, anhydrous butter, whey, lactose or any other
dairy product.

18-20 COOKIES

Sinfully Chocolate Drops

Directions

1. Preheat oven to 325 degrees F.
2. Lightly grease two cookie sheets with canola oil.
3. Melt the 5 ounces of semisweet chocolate and 3 ounces of unsweetened chocolate in a double boiler with the oil. Stir until blended. Remove from heat and allow to cool slightly.
4. Combine the flour, baking powder and salt. Set aside.
5. Blend the eggs, vanilla and coffee granules together with an electric mixer on medium speed.
6. Add the sugar and mix on medium speed until thick.
7. Add the melted chocolate and blend on medium speed.
8. Gradually add the flour mixture on low speed until blended.
9. Add the semisweet chocolate chips and nuts on low speed until combined.
10. Drop large tablespoon sized mounds of the dough about 2 inches apart onto the prepared cookie sheets.
11. Bake for 10-12 minutes at 325 degrees F. The cookies will rise slightly.
12. Immediately remove from the cookie sheets and cool on a wire rack.

Snowcapped Chocolate Mounds

Ingredients

¾ cup unbleached white flour

2 tablespoons *(heaping)* cocoa powder

½ teaspoon baking powder

1 pinch salt

7 ounces semisweet chocolate

⅓ cup canola oil

⅔ cup granulated sugar

3 large eggs, at room temperature

1 tablespoon vanilla extract

1¼ cups confectioner's sugar *(for coating)*

Important: Be sure to read the ingredients list on semisweet chocolate chips and semisweet solid bars for baking. Do not use brands that have butter fat, anhydrous butter, whey, lactose or any other dairy product.

24-30 COOKIES

Snowcapped Chocolate Mounds

Directions

1. Combine the flour, cocoa powder, baking powder and salt. Set aside.
2. Melt the chocolate in a double boiler with the oil. Stir until blended.
3. Remove the mixture from the heat and stir in the sugar until the sugar dissolves.
4. Add the eggs, one at a time, until blended.
5. Stir in the vanilla.
6. Gradually add the flour mixture until blended.
7. Cover the batter and refrigerate for 2-3 hours until the dough is cool and stiff.
8. 15 MINUTES BEFORE BAKING, preheat oven to 325 degrees F.
9. Lightly grease two cookie sheets with canola oil.
10. Pour the confectioner's sugar into a shallow bowl.
11. Form the batter into teaspoon sized balls and roll in the confectioner's sugar until coated.
12. Place on prepared cookie sheets and bake for 10-12 minutes at 325 degrees F.
13. Let cool for 2-3 minutes on the cookie sheets before removing to a wire rack to cool completely.

Turtles

Ingredients

8 ounces bittersweet chocolate

2 tablespoons canola oil

3 tablespoons unbleached white flour

¼ teaspoon baking powder

1 pinch salt

2 large eggs, at room temperature

⅔ cup granulated sugar

1 teaspoon vanilla extract

1½ cups semisweet chocolate chips

2 cups cashew halves

Important: Be sure to read the ingredients list on semisweet chocolate chips. Do not use brands that have butter fat, anhydrous butter, whey, lactose or any other dairy product.

36 COOKIES

Turtles

Directions

1. Preheat oven to 350 degrees F.
2. Line two cookie sheets with foil, shinny side down.
3. Melt the bittersweet chocolate in a double boiler with the oil. Stir until blended. Set aside.
4. Combine the flour, baking powder and salt. Set aside.
5. Blend the eggs, sugar and vanilla with an electric mixer on high speed until light yellow.
6. Using a spatula, fold in the chocolate mixture and then the flour mixture.
7. Stir in the chocolate chips and cashews.
8. Drop tablespoon sized mounds of the dough about 2 inches apart onto the prepared cookie sheets.
9. Bake for 6 minutes at 350 degrees F. Turn the pan 180 degrees and bake for 3-4 minutes more. The tops will look dry.
10. Cool completely on the cookie sheets before removing the cookies or they will fall apart.

IV
Muffins
&
Breads

Apple Streusel Muffins

Ingredients

TOPPING

⅓ cup granulated sugar

2 tablespoons unbleached white flour

1 teaspoon ground cinnamon

1 tablespoon canola oil

BATTER

1 large apple, peeled, cored and cut into ¼-inch chunks

2½ cups unbleached white flour

1 cup granulated sugar

1 tablespoon baking powder

1 teaspoon baking soda

½ teaspoon ground allspice

1 pinch salt

1 cup orange juice

1 large egg, at room temperature

2 large egg whites, at room temperature

2 tablespoons canola oil

2 tablespoons light corn syrup

1 tablespoon vanilla extract

12 muffin papers *(optional)*

12 MUFFINS

Apple Streusel Muffins

Directions

TOPPING

1. Combine all the ingredients in a small bowl and mix together to form coarse crumbs. Set aside.

BATTER

1. Preheat oven to 375 degrees F.
2. Lightly grease 12 muffin cups with canola oil. If using muffin papers, place the papers into the cups and lightly grease the paper cups.
3. Combine the flour, sugar, baking powder, baking soda, allspice and salt. Set aside.
4. Combine the orange juice, egg, egg whites, oil, corn syrup and vanilla. Beat with a fork until blended.
5. Add chopped apple to juice mixture and stir.
6. Make a well in the center of the flour mixture and pour in the orange juice mixture all at once.
7. Mix with a fork until the flour mixture is moist. **DO NOT OVER MIX.**
8. Fill the muffin cups to the rim. Sprinkle the tops with the streusel.
9. Bake for 20 minutes at 375 degrees F. Muffins will be golden brown.
10. Cool on a wire rack for 10 minutes before removing from the pan.

Applesauce Bread

Ingredients

1¾ cups unbleached white flour
¼ teaspoons baking powder
½ teaspoon baking soda
1 pinch salt
½ teaspoon ground cinnamon
½ teaspoon ground clove
½ teaspoon allspice
1½ cup granulated sugar
⅓ cup canola oil
1 large egg, at room temperature
½ cup orange juice
1 cup applesauce
¾ cup chopped raisins
½ cup chopped cashews

12 SERVINGS

Applesauce Bread

Directions

1. Preheat oven to 325 degrees F.
2. Lightly grease (with canola oil) and flour a 4x8-inch loaf pan.
3. Combine the flour, baking powder, baking soda, salt, cinnamon, clove and allspice. Set aside.
4. Blend the sugar and oil together with an electric mixer on medium speed.
5. Add the egg and orange juice and mix on medium speed until blended.
6. Add the applesauce and mix on medium speed until blended.
7. Gradually add the flour mixture on low speed until blended.
8. Add the chopped raisins and cashews on medium speed until blended.
9. Pour the batter into prepared pan. Bake for 55-60 minutes at 325 degrees F. or until the cake is golden brown.
10. Cool on wire rack for ½ hour before removing from the pan.

Banana Nut Bread

Ingredients

2 cups unbleached white flour
1 teaspoon baking soda
1 pinch salt
¾ cup granulated sugar
½ cup canola oil
1 large egg, at room temperature
4 teaspoons lemon juice
1 cup mashed *(2 to 3)* ripe bananas
½ cup cashews, chopped

12 SERVINGS

Banana Nut Bread

Directions

1. Preheat oven to 350 degrees F.
2. Lightly grease (with canola oil) and flour a 4x8-inch loaf pan.
3. Combine the flour, baking soda and salt. Set aside.
4. Blend the sugar and oil together with an electric mixer on medium speed.
5. Gradually add the egg and lemon juice and mix on medium speed until blended.
6. Gradually add the flour mixture on low speed until blended.
7. Add the mashed bananas and nuts on low speed until blended.
8. Pour the batter into prepared pan. Bake for 1 hour at 350 degrees F.
   DO NOT OVER BAKE.
9. Cool on a wire rack for ½ hour before removing from the pan.

Blueberry Muffins

Ingredients

2 cups unbleached white flour
⅓ cup granulated sugar
3 teaspoons baking powder
1 pinch salt
1 cup orange juice
⅓ cup canola oil
1 large egg, at room temperature
2 cups blueberries
12 muffin papers *(optional)*
12 teaspoons granulated sugar *(for sprinkling)*

12 MUFFINS

Blueberry Muffins

Directions

1. Preheat oven to 400 degrees F.
2. Lightly grease 12 muffin cups with canola oil. If using muffin papers, place the papers into the cups and lightly grease the paper cups.
3. Combine the flour, sugar, baking powder and salt. Set aside.
4. Combine the orange juice, oil and egg. Beat with a fork until blended.
5. Make a well in the center of the flour mixture and pour in the orange juice mixture all at once.
6. Mix with a fork until the flour mixture is moist. **DO NOT OVER MIX.**
7. Gently fold in the blueberries.
8. Fill the muffin cups to the rim.
9. Lightly sprinkle the tops with granulated sugar.
10. Bake for 20-25 minutes at 400 degrees F. Muffins will be golden brown.
11. Cool on a wire rack for 10 minutes before removing from pan.

Cherry Muffins

Ingredients

TOPPING

⅓ cup granulated sugar

3 tablespoons unbleached white flour

¼ cup quick cooking oats

2 tablespoons canola oil

BATTER

2½ cups unbleached white flour

1 cup granulated sugar

1 tablespoon baking powder

1 teaspoon baking soda

1 pinch salt

1 cup orange juice

1 large egg, at room temperature

2 large egg whites, at room temperature

2 tablespoons canola oil

4 tablespoons light corn syrup

1 tablespoon vanilla extract

2 cups canned, pitted sour cherries

12 muffin papers *(optional)*

12 MUFFINS

Cherry Muffins

Directions

TOPPING

1. Combine all the ingredients in a small bowl and mix together to form coarse crumbs. Set aside.

BATTER

1. Preheat oven to 375 degrees F.
2. Lightly grease 12 muffin cups with canola oil. If using muffin papers, place the papers into the cups and lightly grease the paper.
3. Combine the flour, sugar, baking powder, baking soda and salt. Set aside.
4. Combine the orange juice, egg, egg whites, oil, corn syrup and vanilla. Beat with a fork until blended.
5. Make a well in the center of the flour mixture and pour in the orange juice mixture all at once.
6. Mix with a fork until the flour mixture is moist.
   DO NOT OVER MIX.
7. Fill the muffin cups within ¼-inch of the rim with the batter. Place about 5-6 cherries on the top of each muffin. Sprinkle the tops with the streusel.
8. Bake for 20 minutes at 375 degrees F. Muffins will be golden brown.
9. Cool on a wire rack for 10 minutes before removing from the pan.

Chocolate Chip Muffins

Ingredients

2½ cups unbleached white flour
1¼ cups granulated sugar
½ cup semisweet chocolate chips
1 tablespoon baking powder
1 teaspoon baking soda
1 pinch salt
1 cup orange juice
1 large egg, at room temperature
2 large egg whites, at room temperature
2 tablespoons canola oil
1 tablespoon vanilla extract
12 muffin papers *(optional)*

Important: Be sure to read the ingredients list on semisweet chocolate chips and semisweet solid bars for baking. Do not use brands that have butter fat, anhydrous butter, whey, lactose or any other dairy product.

12 MUFFINS

Chocolate Chip Muffins

Directions

1. Preheat oven to 375 degrees F.
2. Lightly grease 12 muffin cups with canola oil. If using muffin papers, place the papers into the cups and lightly grease the paper cups.
3. Combine the flour, sugar, chocolate chips, baking powder, baking soda and salt. Set aside.
4. Combine the orange juice, egg, egg whites, oil and vanilla. Beat with a fork until blended.
5. Make a well in the center of the flour mixture and pour in the orange juice mixture all at once.
6. Mix with a fork until the flour mixture is moist. **DO NOT OVER MIX.**
7. Fill the muffin cups to the rim.
8. Bake for 20 minutes at 375 degrees F. Muffins will be golden brown.
9. Cool on a wire rack for 10 minutes before removing from the pan.

Chocolate Cup Cakes

Ingredients

CUP CAKES

2 cups unbleached white flour
4 tablespoons unsweetened cocoa
1 teaspoon baking soda
1 pinch salt
$2/3$ cup canola oil
1¼ cups granulated sugar
3 large eggs, at room temperature
1 cup orange juice
16 cup cake papers

ICING

4 ounces semisweet chocolate
$1/3$ cup canola oil
1½ cups confectioner's sugar

16 CUP CAKES

Chocolate Cup Cakes

Directions

CUP CAKES

1. Preheat oven to 350 degrees F.
2. Line 16 muffin cups with papers. Lightly grease the paper cups.
3. Combine the flour, cocoa, baking soda and salt. Set aside.
4. Combine the oil and sugar together with an electric mixer on high speed until blended.
5. Add the eggs, one at a time, on medium speed until blended.
6. Alternately add the flour mixture and the orange juice on low speed until blended.
7. Fill the muffin cups to the rim.
8. Bake for 15-20 minutes at 350 degrees F. Tops will spring back when touched.
9. Cool on a wire rack for 5 minutes before removing from pan.

ICING

1. Melt the chocolate in a double boiler with the oil. Remove from heat.
2. Gradually add the confectioner's sugar and stir with a fork until blended.
3. Using a spatula, spread the icing evenly over the tops of the cup cakes.

Chocolate Muffins

Ingredients

2½ cups unbleached white flour
1¼ cups granulated sugar
3 tablespoons *(heaping)* unsweetened cocoa
1 tablespoon baking powder
1½ teaspoon ground cinnamon
1 teaspoon baking soda
1 pinch salt
1 cup orange juice
1 large egg, at room temperature
2 large egg whites, at room temperature
2 tablespoons canola oil
1 tablespoon vanilla extract
12 muffin papers *(optional)*

12 MUFFINS

Chocolate Muffins

Directions

1. Preheat oven to 375 degrees F.
2. Lightly grease 12 muffin cups with canola oil. If using muffin papers, place the papers into the cups and lightly grease the paper cups.
3. Combine the flour, sugar, cocoa, baking powder, cinnamon, baking soda and salt. Set aside.
4. Combine the orange juice, egg, egg whites, oil and vanilla. Beat with a fork until blended.
5. Make a well in the center of the flour mixture and pour in the orange juice mixture all at once.
6. Mix with a fork until the flour mixture is moist. **DO NOT OVER MIX.**
7. Fill the muffin cups to the rim.
8. Bake for 20 minutes at 375 degrees F. Muffins will be golden brown.
9. Cool on a wire rack for 10 minutes before removing from the pan.

Cinnamon Muffins

Ingredients

TOPPING

⅓ cup granulated sugar

2 tablespoons unbleached white flour

1 teaspoon ground cinnamon

1 tablespoon canola oil

BATTER

2½ cups unbleached white flour

1 cup granulated sugar

1 tablespoon baking powder

1 teaspoon baking soda

1 teaspoon ground cinnamon

1 pinch salt

1 cup orange juice

1 large egg, at room temperature

2 large egg whites, at room temperature

2 tablespoons canola oil

2 tablespoons light corn syrup

1 tablespoon vanilla extract

12 muffin papers *(optional)*

12 MUFFINS

Cinnamon Muffins

Directions

TOPPING

1. Combine all the ingredients in a small bowl and mix together to form coarse crumbs. Set aside.

BATTER

1. Preheat oven to 375 degrees F.
2. Lightly grease 12 muffin cups with canola oil. If using muffin papers, place the papers into the cups and lightly grease the paper cups.
3. Combine the flour, sugar, baking powder, baking soda, cinnamon and salt. Set aside.
4. Combine the orange juice, egg, egg whites, oil, corn syrup and vanilla. Beat with a fork until blended.
5. Make a well in the center of the flour mixture and pour in the orange juice mixture all at once.
6. Mix with a fork until the flour mixture is moist.
   DO NOT OVER MIX.
7. Fill the muffin cups to the rim.
8. Sprinkle the tops with the streusel.
9. Bake for 20 minutes at 375 degrees F. Muffins will be golden brown.
10. Cool on a wire rack for 10 minutes before removing from the pan.

Cranberry Bread

Ingredients

2 cups unbleached white flour
1 cup granulated sugar
1½ teaspoons baking powder
½ teaspoon baking soda
1 pinch salt
1 orange, grated and squeezed
½ cup boiling water
1 large egg, at room temperature
2 tablespoons canola oil
1 cup fresh cranberries
½ cup chopped cashews

12 SERVINGS

Cranberry Bread

Directions

1. Preheat oven to 325 degrees F.
2. Lightly grease (with canola oil) and flour a 4x8-inch loaf pan.
3. Combine the flour, sugar, baking powder, baking soda and salt. Set aside.
4. Put the juice and grated rind of the orange into a measuring cup. Add enough boiling water to measure ¾ of a cup.
5. Pour the orange mixture into the flour mixture. Mix until blended.
6. Beat egg and oil together with a fork and add to the batter. Mix until blended.
7. Add cranberries and nuts to the batter. Mix until blended.
8. Pour the batter into the prepared pan. Bake for 45-50 minutes at 325 degrees F. Cake will be golden brown.
9. Cool completely on a wire rack before removing from pan.
10. Best when stored 24 hours before serving.

Cranberry Muffins

Ingredients

2 cups unbleached white flour
⅓ cup granulated sugar
3 teaspoons baking powder
1 pinch salt
1 cup orange juice
⅓ cup canola oil
1 large egg, at room temperature
2 cups cranberries
12 muffin papers *(optional)*

12 MUFFINS

Cranberry Muffins

Directions

1. Preheat oven to 400 degrees F.
2. Lightly grease 12 muffin cups with canola oil. If using muffin papers, place the papers into the cups and lightly grease the paper cups.
3. Combine the flour, sugar, baking powder and salt. Set aside.
4. Combine the orange juice, oil and egg. Beat with a fork until blended.
5. Make a well in the center of the flour mixture and pour in the orange juice mixture all at once.
6. Mix with a fork until the flour mixture is moist. **DO NOT OVER MIX.**
7. Fold in the cranberries.
8. Fill the muffin cups to the rim.
9. Lightly sprinkle the tops with granulated sugar.
10. Bake for 20-25 minutes at 400 degrees F. Muffins will be golden brown.
11. Cool on a wire rack for 10 minutes before removing from the pan.

Date Nut Bread

Ingredients

8 ounces dried dates
1 cup chopped cashews
1¼ cups boiling water
1½ teaspoons baking soda
1 large egg, separated, at room temperature
1 teaspoon vanilla
2 cups unbleached white flour
¾ cup granulated sugar

12 SERVINGS

Date Nut Bread

Directions

1. Preheat oven to 350 degrees F.

2. Lightly grease (with canola oil) and flour a 4x8-inch loaf pan.

3. Chop dates and nuts into small pieces.

4. Combine the boiling water and baking soda and pour over the dates and nuts. Cool to room temperature.

5. Combine the egg yolk and vanilla and add to the cooled date-nut mixture.

6. Gradually add the flour to the date-nut mixture until blended.

7. Beat the egg white with an electric mixer on high speed until frothed. Gradually add the sugar and continue beating until the egg whites form stiff peaks (about 1 minute).

8. Using a spatula, gently fold the egg whites into the date-nut mixture.

9. Pour the batter into the prepared pan. Bake for 1 hour at 350 degrees F. Cake will spring back to touch.

10. Cool on a wire rack for ½ hour before removing from the pan.

Lemon Iced Bread

Ingredients

BREAD

1½ cups unbleached white flour

2 teaspoons baking powder

1 cup granulated sugar

½ cup canola oil

2 large eggs, at room temperature

½ cup orange juice

1 tablespoon lemon juice

2 tablespoons lemon zest

FROSTING

2 cups confectioner's sugar

1½ tablespoons canola oil

1 tablespoon lemon zest

3 tablespoons lemon juice

2 tablespoons orange juice

12 SERVINGS

Lemon Iced Bread

Directions

BREAD

1. Preheat oven to 350 degrees F.
2. Lightly grease (with canola oil) and flour a 4x8-inch loaf pan.
3. Combine the flour and baking powder. Set aside.
4. Blend the sugar and oil together with an electric mixer on medium speed until combined.
5. Add the eggs, one at a time, on medium speed until blended.
6. Add the orange juice, lemon juice and lemon zest on medium speed until blended.
7. Gradually add the flour mixture on low speed until blended.
8. Pour the batter into the prepared pan. Bake for 45-50 minutes at 350 degrees F. or until a toothpick comes out clean.
9. Cool completely on a wire rack before removing from the pan.

FROSTING

1. Combine the confectioner's sugar, oil, lemon zest and gradually add enough of the lemon and orange juice to make a soft icing.
2. Spread frosting over cooled cake.

Lemon Poppy Seed Muffins

Ingredients

2½ cups unbleached white flour
1 cup granulated sugar
1½ tablespoons poppy seeds
1 tablespoon baking powder
1 pinch salt
1 cup orange juice
¼ cup lemon juice
1 large egg, at room temperature
2 large egg whites, at room temperature
2 tablespoons lemon zest
2 tablespoons canola oil
1 tablespoon vanilla extract
12 muffin papers *(optional)*

12 MUFFINS

Lemon Poppy Seed Muffins

Directions

1. Preheat oven to 375 degrees F.
2. Lightly grease 12 muffin cups with canola oil. If using muffin papers, place the papers into the cups and lightly grease the paper cups.
3. Combine the flour, sugar, poppy seeds, baking powder and salt. Set aside.
4. Combine the orange juice, lemon juice, egg, egg whites, lemon zest, oil and vanilla. Beat with a fork until blended.
5. Make a well in the center of the flour mixture and pour in the orange juice mixture all at once.
6. Mix with a fork until the flour mixture is moist.
   DO NOT OVER MIX.
7. Fill the muffin cups to the rim.
8. Bake for 20 minutes at 375 degrees F. Muffins will be golden brown.
9. Cool on a wire rack for 10 minutes before removing from the pan.

Lemonade Bread

Ingredients

CAKE

1½ cups unbleached white flour

2 teaspoons baking powder

1 cup granulated sugar

½ cup canola oil

2 large eggs, at room temperature

½ cup orange juice

1 tablespoon frozen lemonade concentrate, thawed

TOPPING

⅓ cup frozen lemonade concentrate, thawed

12 SERVINGS

Lemonade Bread

Directions

~~◦~~

CAKE

1. Preheat oven to 350 degrees F.
2. Lightly grease (with canola oil) and flour a 4x8-inch loaf pan.
3. Combine the flour and baking powder. Set aside.
4. Blend the sugar and oil together with an electric mixer on medium speed.
5. Add the eggs, one at a time, on medium speed until blended.
6. Add the orange juice and lemonade concentrate on medium speed until blended.
7. Gradually add the flour mixture on low speed until blended.
8. Pour the batter into the prepared pan. Bake for 45-50 minutes at 350 degrees F. Toothpick will come out clean.

TOPPING

1. Pour 1/3 cup of lemonade concentrate over the hot bread.
2. Cool completely on a wire rack before removing from the pan.

Orange Bread

Ingredients

BREAD

1¾ cups unbleached white flour

2 teaspoons baking powder

1 pinch salt

1 cup granulated sugar

½ cup canola oil

2 large eggs, separated, at room temperature

½ cup orange juice

¾ cup chopped raisins

2 tablespoons orange zest

FROSTING

1 cup confectioner's sugar

1½ tablespoons canola oil

1 tablespoon orange zest

3 tablespoons lemon juice

2 tablespoons orange juice

12 SERVINGS

Orange Bread

Directions

~⌐

BREAD

1. Preheat oven to 350 degrees F.
2. Lightly grease (with canola oil) and flour a 4x8-inch loaf pan.
3. Combine the flour, baking powder and salt. Set aside.
4. Blend the sugar and oil together with an electric mixer on medium speed until smooth.
5. Add the egg yolks and orange juice and mix on medium speed until blended.
6. Gradually add the flour mixture on low speed until blended.
7. Add the chopped raisins and orange zest on medium speed until blended.
8. Beat the egg whites on high speed until stiff peaks form. Fold the egg whites into the batter with a spatula.
9. Pour the batter into the prepared pan. Bake for 50-60 minutes at 350 degrees F. The cake will be golden brown.
10. Cool on wire rack before removing from pan.

FROSTING

1. Combine the confectioner's sugar, oil, orange zest and gradually add enough of the lemon and orange juice to make a soft icing. Spread frosting over cooled cake.

Orange Poppy Seed Muffins with Almond

Ingredients

2½ cups unbleached white flour

1 cup granulated sugar

2½ tablespoons poppy seeds

1 tablespoon baking powder

1 pinch salt

¾ cup orange juice

1 large egg, at room temperature

2 large egg whites, at room temperature

2 tablespoons canola oil

1 tablespoon vanilla extract

1½ teaspoons almond extract

2 tablespoons orange zest

12 muffin papers *(optional)*

12 MUFFINS

Orange Poppy Seed Muffins with Almond

Directions

1. Preheat oven to 375 degrees F.
2. Lightly grease 12 muffin cups with canola oil. If using muffin papers, place the papers into the cups and lightly grease the paper cups.
3. Combine the flour, sugar, poppy seeds, baking powder and salt. Set aside.
4. Combine the orange juice, egg, egg whites, oil, vanilla, almond extract and orange zest. Beat with a fork until blended.
5. Make a well in the center of the flour mixture and pour in the orange juice mixture all at once.
6. Mix with a fork until the flour mixture is moist. **DO NOT OVER MIX.**
7. Fill the muffin cups to the rim.
8. Bake for 20 minutes at 375 degrees F. Muffins will be golden brown.
9. Cool on a wire rack for 10 minutes before removing from the pan.

Pineapple Down-under Muffins

Ingredients

BATTER

2 cups unbleached white flour

4 tablespoons granulated sugar

1 tablespoon baking powder

1 pinch salt

1 cup pineapple juice

¼ cup canola oil

2 large eggs, at room temperature

BOTTOM

12 teaspoons light brown sugar *(lightly packed)*

12 teaspoons cashews, coarsely chopped

1 cup crushed pineapple, drained, with juice reserved

6 teaspoons granulated sugar *(for sprinkling)*

12 muffin papers

12 MUFFINS

Pineapple Down-under Muffins

Directions

~<>

BATTER

1. Preheat oven to 400 degrees F.
2. Place 12 muffin papers into the muffin cups and lightly grease the papers with canola oil.
3. Combine the flour, sugar, baking powder and salt. Set aside.
4. Combine pineapple juice, oil and eggs. Beat with a fork until blended.
5. Make a well in the center of the flour mixture and pour in the pineapple juice mixture all at once.
6. Mix with a fork until the flour mixture is moist.
   DO NOT OVER MIX.

BOTTOM

1. In the bottom of each muffin cup place 1 teaspoon brown sugar, 1 teaspoon nuts and 2 tablespoons crushed pineapple.
2. Fill the muffin cups to the rim.
3. Sprinkle the top of each muffin with ½ teaspoon granulated sugar.
4. Bake for 20-25 minutes at 400 degrees F. Muffins will be golden brown.
5. Cool on a wire rack for 10 minutes before removing from the pan.

Pumpkin Muffins

Ingredients

2½ cups unbleached white flour
½ cup granulated sugar
½ cup light brown sugar *(firmly packed)*
1 tablespoon baking powder
1 teaspoon baking soda
1 teaspoon ground nutmeg
1 teaspoon ground cinnamon
1 teaspoon ground ginger
1 pinch salt
¾ cup orange juice
½ cup canned pumpkin
1 large egg, at room temperature
1 large egg whites, at room temperature
2 tablespoons canola oil
1 tablespoon vanilla extract
12 muffin papers *(optional)*

12 MUFFINS

Pumpkin Muffins

Directions

1. Preheat oven to 375 degrees F.
2. Lightly grease 12 muffin cups with canola oil. If using muffin papers, place the papers into the cups and lightly grease the paper cups.
3. Combine the flour, both sugars, baking powder, baking soda, nutmeg, cinnamon, ginger and salt. Set aside.
4. Combine the orange juice, pumpkin, egg, egg white, oil and vanilla. Beat with a fork until blended.
5. Make a well in the center of the flour mixture and pour in the orange juice mixture all at once.
6. Mix with a fork until the flour mixture is moist. **DO NOT OVER MIX.**
7. Fill the muffin cups to the rim.
8. Bake for 20 minutes at 375 degrees F. Muffins will be golden brown.
9. Cool on a wire rack for 10 minutes before removing from the pan.

Scones

Ingredients

BATTER

2 cups unbleached white flour

1 tablespoon baking powder

1 pinch salt

1¼ cups orange juice

3 tablespoons canola oil

¼ cup granulated sugar *(for sprinkling)*

FILLING

¾ cup semisweet chocolate chips

      OR

2 medium apples, peeled, corded, cut into ½-inch chunks
and tossed in 1 tablespoon cinnamon

      OR

¾ cup blueberries

12 SCONES

Scones

Directions

1. Preheat oven to 425 degrees F.
2. Set aside a heavy baking sheet.
3. Combine the flour, baking powder and salt. Toss with a fork until blended.
4. Add the filling of choice and mix with a fork until blended.
5. Add the orange juice and mix with a fork until blended. The batter will be sticky.
6. Transfer the dough to a floured surface. Knead the dough until it sets.
7. Form the dough into a 9-inch disk.
8. Lightly brush the dough with the canola oil. Sprinkle the dough with granulated sugar. *(When using the apple filling, also sprinkle the dough with cinnamon.)*
9. Cut the dough into 12 pie shaped sections. Carefully place the separated slices on to the cookie sheet. Leave a 2 inch space between each piece.
10. Bake for 15-17 minutes at 425 degrees F. The tops will be golden brown.
11. Scones are best served hot or at room temperature with jam on the day they are baked.

V

Pies
&
Tarts
&
Cobblers

Apple Tart

Ingredients

CRUST

1 double Basic Tart Crust *(pages 196-197)*

FILLING

¼ cup canola oil
¼ cup granulated sugar
1 pinch salt
6 large apples, peeled, cored and cut into ¼-inch slices

TOPPING

2 tablespoons confectioner's sugar *(for sprinkling)*

12-14 SERVINGS

Apple Tart

Directions

CRUST

1. Make the tart crust. Press 1 crust into an 11-inch tart pan. Prebake and allow to cool. Wrap 2nd crust in plastic wrap and refrigerate.

FILLING

1. Preheat oven to 425 degrees F.
2. Heat the oil, sugar and salt in a large skillet until it starts to caramelize.
3. Add the apples and sauté until the apples soften.
4. Spread the apples mixture over the baked tart shell.
5. Crumble the 2nd crust over the apples.
6. Bake for 30-35 minutes at 425 degrees F. The top will be golden brown.
7. Cool on a wire rack for 15 minutes before removing the side of the pan. Sprinkle with confectioner's sugar when cool.

4th of July Apple Pie

Ingredients

CRUST

1 double Basic Pie Crust *(pages 194-195)*

FILLING

12 large apples, peeled, cored and cut into ½ inch slices
¾ cup granulated sugar
1½ teaspoons ground cinnamon
½ teaspoon ground nutmeg
1 pinch salt
¼ cup orange juice
2 tablespoons lemon juice
1½ tablespoons cornstarch
1 tablespoon oil

GLAZE

1 large egg, at room temperature
2 tablespoons water

8-12 SERVINGS

4th of July Apple Pie

Directions

CRUST

1. Make the pie crust. Place 1 crust into a 9-inch pie plate. Roll out the 2nd crust. Wrap both crusts in plastic wrap and refrigerate.

FILLING

1. Preheat oven to 450 degrees F.

2. Combine the apple slices and all of the other ingredients EXCEPT the glaze.

3. Toss the mixture together by hand until all of the apple slices are evenly coated.

4. Sauté the apples in a large skillet until soft.

5. Spread the apple mixture over the bottom pie crust.

6. Cover the apples with the top crust.

7. Seal and trim the edges.

8. Whisk together the egg and water for the glaze.

9. Make 3 to 4 slits in the top crust and brush the top with the egg glaze.

10. Bake for 20 minutes at 450 degrees F.

11. Reduce the temperature of the oven to 350 degrees F. and bake for 50-60 minutes. The top of the crust will be golden brown and the apple filling will be bubbly. Cool on a wire rack.

Cape Cod Cranberry & Apple Tart

Ingredients

CRUST

1 single Basic Tart Crust *(pages 196-197)*

FILLING

5 large apples, cored, peeled and cut into ½-inch cubes
½ cup light brown sugar *(lightly packed)*
1 tablespoon orange zest
2 pinches salt
1 teaspoon cornstarch
⅓ cup orange juice
2 cups fresh Cape Cod cranberries

TOPPING

¾ cup unbleached white flour
½ cup chopped cashews
½ cup light brown sugar *(lightly packed)*
½ cup quick cooking oats
½ teaspoon ground cinnamon
½ cup canola oil

12-14 SERVINGS

Cape Cod Cranberry & Apple Tart

Directions

CRUST

1. Make the tart crust. Press the crust into 9-inch tart pan. Prebake and allow to cool.

FILLING

1. Preheat oven to 400 degrees F.
2. Combine the sliced apples, sugar, orange zest and salt in a large sauté pan and toss.
3. Dissolve the cornstarch in the orange juice. Add to the apple mixture and toss.
4. Cover and simmer the apple mixture on medium-low heat for 4-6 minutes. Stir every 2 minutes.
5. Stir the cranberries into the apple mixture, cover and continue to simmer on medium-low heat for 5 minutes more.
6. Remove cranberry-apple mixture from heat and spread over the baked tart shell.

TOPPING

1. Combine all the ingredients in a large bowl and toss together.
2. Spread the topping over the cranberry-apple mixture in the tart shell.
3. Bake for 15 minutes at 400 degrees F.
4. Lightly cover the tart with foil (do not seal) and bake for 30 minutes more.
5. Cool on a wire rack for an hour before serving.

Geo. Washington Cherry Tart

Ingredients

CRUST

1 double Basic Tart Crust *(pages 196-197)*

FILLING

1½ tablespoons cornstarch
1 cup cherry juice *(from the canned cherries)*
½ cup light brown sugar *(lightly packed)*
1½ teaspoons grated orange zest
1 teaspoon ground cinnamon
¼ teaspoon ground mace
1 pinch salt
4 cups drained canned sour cherries
2 tablespoons quick cooking oats

12-14 SERVINGS

Geo. Washington Cherry Tart

Directions

❧

CRUST

1. Make the tart crust. Place 1 crust into an 11-inch tart pan. Wrap both crusts in plastic wrap and refrigerate

FILLING

1. Preheat oven to 400 degrees F.
2. Dissolve the cornstarch in ⅓ cup cherry juice.
3. Combine ⅔ cup cherry juice, sugar, orange zest, cinnamon, mace and salt in a medium sauce pan and bring to a boil over medium-low heat.
4. Stirring vigorously with a whisk, combine the cherry juice mixture over medium-low heat.
5. Boil for 5 minutes or until the mixture thickens.
6. Pour the juice mixture over the cherries and toss.
7. Remove the tart crusts from the refrigerator.
8. Sprinkle the oats over the bottom of the crust in the tart pan.
9. Spread the cherries over the oats.
10. Crumble the 2nd crust over the cherries.
11. Place the tart on a cookie sheet and bake for 45 minutes at 400 degrees F. The top crust will be golden brown.
12. Remove the tart from the oven and cool on a wire rack for an hour.
13. Push the bottom of the tart pan up to prevent the filling from sticking to the edges.
14. Cool for 4-5 hours before serving.

Granny Smith's Apples Cobbled

Ingredients

FILLING

6 Granny Smith apples, peeled, cored and cut into ½-inch slices

5 tablespoons granulated sugar

TOPPING

²/₃ cup unbleached white flour

²/₃ cup light brown sugar *(lightly packed)*

²/₃ cup finely chopped cashews

½ teaspoon ground cinnamon

¹/₃ cup canola oil

8-10 SERVINGS

Granny Smith's Apples Cobbled

Directions

FILLING

1. Preheat oven to 350 degrees F.
2. Lightly grease an 8-inch square baking pan with canola oil.
3. Spread half of the apple slices in the prepared pan.
4. Sprinkle apples with granulated sugar.
5. Spread the remaining apples over the sugar.

TOPPING

1. Combine the flour, brown sugar, cashews and cinnamon in a large bowl and mix.
2. Using a wooden spoon, blend the oil into flour mixture.
3. Spread topping over the apples.
4. Bake for 55-60 minutes at 350 degrees F. The top will be golden brown and crunchy. The filling will be bubbly. Serve hot.

Patrick Hart's Kiwi & Strawberry Tart

Ingredients

CUSTARD

3 tablespoons cornstarch

1 cup water

2 large eggs, at room temperature

¾ cup granulated sugar

1 pinch salt

⅓ cup lemon juice

CRUST

1 single Basic Tart Crust *(pages 196-197)*

TOPPING

2 pints fresh strawberries, washed and hulled

3 ripe kiwis, peeled and slices

1 pint fresh blueberries, washed and drained

GLAZE

3 ounces apple jelly

12-14 SERVINGS

Patrick Hart's Kiwi & Strawberry Tart

Directions

~~⌒~~

CUSTARD

1. Dissolve the cornstarch in ½ cup water.
2. Add the eggs and whisk until blended.
3. Combine ½ cup water, sugar and salt in a small sauce pan and heat until the sugar dissolves.
4. Add cornstarch mixture to the hot liquid, stir constantly.
5. Add lemon juice, stir constantly for 3 or 4 minutes. Mixture will thicken. Cook for 1 minute more.
6. Remove custard from heat and pour into a bowl through a sieve to remove any cooked egg.
7. Cover custard with plastic wrap. Refrigerate.

CRUST

1. Make the tart crust. Press the crust into a 9-inch tart pan. Prebake and allow to cool.

TOPPING

1. Spread all the custard evenly over the crust.
2. Prepare fruit. Arrange over the custard. *(Be creative!)*

GLAZE

1. Heat the apple jelly in a small saucepan until liquid.
2. Using a pastry brush, coat the fruit with the jelly. Refrigerate for 1 hour before serving.

Puff Pastry
(Cover Recipe)

Ingredients

SHELLS

1 cup water
½ cup canola oil
1 pinch salt
1 cup unbleached white flour
4 large eggs, at room temperature

FILLING

2 Lemon Custard Filling recipes *(pages 222-223)*

TOPPING

1 Chocolate Icing recipe *(pages 220-221)*

6 SERVINGS

Puff Pastry
(Cover Recipe)

Directions

PASTRY

1. Preheat oven to 450 degrees F.
2. Lightly grease two cookie sheets with canola oil.
3. Combine the water, canola oil and salt in a medium saucepan and bring to a boil.
4. Remove the mixture from the heat and stir in the flour ALL AT ONCE. Stir vigorously until the flour mixture pulls away from the side of the pan and forms a ball. Add a little heat if the flour mixture does not form a ball almost immediately.
5. Add the eggs, one at a time, and combine until the mixture is smooth and glossy after each egg.
6. Drop mounds the size of two tablespoons 2 inches apart on to the prepared cookie sheets.
7. Bake for 15 minutes at 450 degrees F. Turn the oven down to 350 degrees F. and bake 25-30 minutes more. The side of the puffs will feel firm. The tops will be golden brown.
8. Cool on a wire rack for 15 minutes before assembly.

ASSEMBLY

1. Slice the cap off of each pastry puff.
2. Spoon about 3-4 tablespoons of the Lemon Custard on to the bottom of each pastry puff.
3. Replace the caps.
4. Spoon 2-3 tablespoons of the Chocolate Icing over each assembled puff and serve.

Lemon Meringue Pie

Ingredients

CRUST

1 single Basic Pie Crust *(pages 194-195)*

FILLING

1½ cups water
¾ cup granulated sugar
6 tablespoons cornstarch
¾ cup lemon juice
3 large egg yolks, at room temperature
3 tablespoons canola oil
1½ teaspoons lemon zest

TOPPING

5 large egg whites, at room temperature
½ cup granulated sugar
½ teaspoon cream of tartar

8-12 SERVINGS

Lemon Meringue Pie

Directions

CRUST

1. Make the pie crust. Place the crust into a 9-inch pie plate. Prebake and allow to cool.

FILLING

1. Combine the water, sugar and cornstarch in a med. sauce pan and cook over medium-low heat for 6-8 minutes or until the mixture thickens.

2. Add the lemon juice and egg yolks and cook over medium-low heat for about 3 minutes or until the egg yolks cook.

3. Strain the mixture into a medium size bowl.

4. Add the oil and lemon zest and stir until blended.

5. Allow the mixture to cool for 10 minutes before spreading the lemon mixture into the baked pie shell. Refrigerate for 4 to 6 hours.

TOPPING

1. Preheat oven to 350 degrees F.

2. Beat the egg whites on medium-high speed until frothed. Gradually add the sugar and cream of tartar and continue beating until the meringue forms stiff peaks (about 1½ minutes).

3. Spread the meringue over the pie making peaks.

4. Bake for 15 minutes at 350 degrees F. The tips and edges of the meringue will be golden brown.

5. Remove the pie from the oven. Cool on a wire rack for 1 hour. Cool in the refrigerator for another hour before serving. Cut with a sharp, hot, dry knife. Best eaten the same day.

Little Jack Horner Plum & Blueberry Pie

Ingredients

CRUST

1 single Basic Pie Crust *(pages 194-195)*

TOPPING

6 tablespoons light brown sugar *(lightly packed)*
¾ cup unbleached white flour
½ cup quick cooking oatmeal
½ cup ground cashews
¼ teaspoon ground cinnamon
½ cup canola oil

FILLING

3 cups fresh blueberries
8 red plums, pitted and sliced into ¾-inch thick slices
½ cup granulated sugar
¼ teaspoon grated orange zest
1 heaping tablespoon cornstarch
2 tablespoons orange juice

8-12 SERVINGS

Little Jack Horner Plum
& Blueberry Pie

Directions

CRUST

1. Make the pie crust. Place the pie crust into a 9-inch pie plate. Prebake and allow to cool.

TOPPING

1. Combine the sugar, flour, oatmeal, nuts and cinnamon in a medium sized bowl. Add the oil and mix until blended. Set aside.

FILLING

1. Preheat oven to 400 degrees F.
2. Combine the fruit, sugar and orange zest in a large bowl and toss.
3. Dissolve the cornstarch in the orange juice and pour over the fruit and toss.
4. Spread the fruit mixture over the pie shell.
5. Spread the topping over the fruit.
6. Place the pie on a cookie sheet and bake for 20 minutes at 400 degrees F.
7. Reduce the temperature of the oven to 350 degrees F. and bake for about 1 hour. The filling will be bubbly.
8. Cool on a wire rack for 3 hours before serving.

Luscious Peach Pie

Ingredients

CRUST

1 single Basic Pie Crust *(pages 194-195)*

TOPPING

1 cup unbleached white flour
½ cup light brown sugar *(lightly packed)*
1 tablespoon ground cinnamon
1 pinch salt
½ cup canola oil

FILLING

8 peaches, peeled, pitted and cut into ¾-inch slices
  (Optional: In the off season this pie can be made with
  canned peaches. Use 2 29-ounce cans of peach halves.
  Drain and cut into slices.)
½ cup granulated sugar
½ teaspoon ground cinnamon
1 pinch salt
1 tablespoon cornstarch
3 tablespoons lemon juice
2 tablespoons orange juice

8-10 SERVINGS

Luscious Peach Pie

Directions

~⌒

CRUST

1. Make the pie crust. Place the crust into a 9-inch pie plate. Prebake and allow to cool.

TOPPING

1. Combine the flour, brown sugar, cinnamon and salt in a medium bowl. Add the oil and mix until blended. Set aside.

FILLING

1. Preheat oven to 400 degrees F.
2. Combine the peaches, sugar, cinnamon and salt in a large bowl and toss.
3. Dissolve the cornstarch in the lemon and orange juices and pour over the fruit and toss.
4. Spread the fruit mixture over the baked pie shell.
5. Spread the topping over the fruit.
6. Place the pie on a cookie sheet and bake for 15 minutes at 400 degrees F.
7. Reduce the temperature of the oven to 350 degrees F. and bake for one hour. The filling will be bubbly.
8. Cool on a wire rack for 3 hours before serving.

Pear & Cranberry Cobbler

Ingredients

FILLING

6 medium sized pears, peeled, cored and cut into ½-inch
  chunks

1 tablespoon canola oil

⅓ cup light brown sugar *(lightly packed)*

⅓ cup granulated sugar

3 tablespoons cornstarch

2 tablespoons lemon juice

2 teaspoons cinnamon

2 teaspoons nutmeg

1 cup fresh or frozen cranberries

TOPPING

1 cup unbleached white flour

¼ cup granulated sugar

1 teaspoon baking powder

2 tablespoons orange juice

1 large egg, at room temperature

¼ cup canola oil

8-10 SERVINGS

Pear & Cranberry Cobbler

Directions

FILLING

1. Preheat oven to 325 degrees F.
2. Lightly grease a 2-quart casserole dish with canola oil.
3. Sauté the pear in the oil until softened. Remove from heat.
4. Add both sugars, cornstarch, lemon juice, cinnamon and nutmeg to the pears. Stir until blended.
5. Add the cranberries and stir until mixed.
6. Pour into prepared pan. Set aside.

TOPPING

1. Combine the flour, sugar and baking powder in a large bowl.
2. Add the orange juice, then the egg and then the oil to flour mixture and blend. Do not over work the batter.
3. Spread the topping over the pear/cranberry mixture.
4. Bake for 55-60 minutes at 325 degrees F. The top will be golden brown. The filling will be bubbly. Serve hot.

Pecan Pie

Ingredients

CRUST

1 single Basic Pie Crust *(pages 194-195)*

FILLING

1 cup granulated sugar
1½ cups dark corn syrup
½ cup canola oil
1 pinch salt
4 large eggs, beaten lightly, at room temperature
½ teaspoon vanilla extract
2 cups pecan halves

8-12 SERVINGS

Pecan Pie

Directions

CRUST

1. Make the pie crust. Place the crust into a 9-inch pie plate. Wrap in plastic wrap and refrigerate.

FILLING

1. Preheat oven to 350 degrees F.
2. Combine the sugar and corn syrup in a small sauce pan and heat over low heat until the sugar is dissolved, stirring occasionally.
3. Remove from heat and add the oil and salt. Allow to cool for 10 minutes.
4. Add the eggs and vanilla to the cooled mixture.
5. Stirring vigorously with a whisk, add the pecans.
6. Spread the pecan mixture over the pie shell.
7. Bake for 50-55 minutes at 350 degrees F. The filling will set and the top will be crisp.
8. Cool completely on a wire rack. This pie is best eaten the next day.

Pecan-Caramel-Coconut Tart

Ingredients

CRUST

1 single Basic Tart Crust *(pages 196-197)*

FILLING

¾ cup light brown sugar *(firmly packed)*
½ cup light corn syrup
½ cup dark corn syrup
3 large egg whites, at room temperature
1 teaspoon vanilla extract
1 pinch salt
2 tablespoons unbleached white flour
½ teaspoon ground allspice
¾ cup shredded coconut
⅓ cup chopped pecans

12-14 SERVINGS

Pecan-Caramel-Coconut Tart

Directions

CRUST

1. Make the tart crust. Press the crust into a 9-inch tart pan. Prebake and allow to cool.

FILLING

1. Preheat oven to 350 degrees F.
2. Combine brown sugar, both corn syrups, egg whites, vanilla and salt in a medium size bowl and whisk together until smooth.
3. Add the flour and allspice and blend.
4. Stir in the coconut and pecans.
5. Spread the pecan mixture over the prepared tart shell.
6. Bake for 30-35 minutes at 350 degrees F. Filling will set.
7. Cool completely on a wire rack before removing the sides of the pan.

Pumpkin Pie

Ingredients

CRUST

1 single Basic Pie Crust *(pages 194-195)*

FILLING

3 large eggs, at room temperature
1 cup light brown sugar *(lightly packed)*
¼ cup granulated sugar
1 teaspoon pumpkin spice
1 teaspoon cinnamon
¼ teaspoon ground cloves
¼ teaspoon nutmeg
¼ teaspoon ground ginger
1 pinch salt
15 ounces pumpkin
2 tablespoons cornstarch
1 cup orange juice

8-12 SERVINGS

Pumpkin Pie

Directions

><

CRUST

1. Make the pie crust. Place the crust into a 9-inch pie plate. Prebake and allow to cool.

FILLING

1. Preheat oven to 450 degrees F.
2. Blend eggs, both sugars, pumpkin spice, cinnamon, ground cloves, nutmeg, ginger and salt together with an electric mixer on medium speed until smooth.
3. Add the pumpkin on medium speed and blend.
4. Dissolve the cornstarch in the orange juice.
5. Add the orange juice mixture on medium speed and blend.
6. Pour the filling into the prepared pie shell.
7. Place the pie on a cookie sheet and bake for 10 minutes at 450 degrees F.
8. Reduce the temperature of the oven to 350 degrees F. and bake for 45-50 minutes. The pie is done when a knife, inserted in the center of the pie, comes out clean.
9. Cool completely on a wire rack.

Rhubarb-Strawberry Cobbler

Ingredients

FILLING

1¼ pounds rhubarb cut into 1-inch chunks

½ cup granulated sugar

1 tablespoon cornstarch

½ cup water

1 pint strawberries, hulled and cut into quarters

TOPPING

1½ cups unbleached white flour

¼ cup granulated sugar

1½ teaspoons baking powder

½ teaspoon baking soda

¼ teaspoon ground cinnamon

⅛ teaspoon ground nutmeg

1 pinch salt

¼ cup canola oil

¾ cup orange juice

1 tablespoon granulated sugar *(for sprinkling)*

8-10 SERVINGS

Rhubarb-Strawberry Cobbler

Directions

FILLING

1. Preheat oven to 400 degrees F.
2. Stirring constantly, combine rhubarb and ½ cup sugar in a medium sauce pan and bring to a boil over medium-high heat. Reduce heat to medium-low, cover and let simmer until rhubarb is tender (about 10 minutes).
3. Combine cornstarch with ½ cup water and blend.
4. Add cornstarch mixture and strawberries to the rhubarb mixture and cook for 2 minutes or until mixture thickens. Remove from heat and pour into a 2 quart casserole.

TOPPING

1. Combine the flour, sugar, baking powder, baking soda, cinnamon, nutmeg and salt in a bowl.
2. Add oil and toss until mixture resembles coarse crumbs.
3. Add the orange juice and mix just until the mixture forms a soft dough.
4. Turn the dough on to a lightly floured surface and knead to mix thoroughly.
5. Roll the dough out to ½ -inch thick. Cut as many 3-inch shapes as will fit with a cookie cutter. Reroll and cut more shapes to make 8 biscuits.
6. Place biscuits on top of rhubarb and sprinkle with the tablespoon of sugar.
7. Place the cobbler on a cookie sheet and bake 20 minutes on 400 degrees F. Biscuits will be golden brown and the filling will be bubbly.
8. Cool for ½ hour on a wire rack. Serve warm.

Sweet-Tart Raisin & Lemon Pie

Ingredients

CRUST

1 single Basic Pie Crust *(pages 194-195)*

FILLING

1¼ cup golden raisins
½ cup lemon juice
1 tablespoon lemon zest
¾ cup chopped cashews
½ cup canola oil
⅓ cup granulated sugar
⅓ cup light brown sugar *(lightly packed)*
¾ teaspoon ground cinnamon
1 pinch salt
3 large eggs, at room temperature

8-12 SERVINGS

Sweet-Tart Raisin & Lemon Pie

Directions

CRUST

1. Make the pie crust. Place the crust into a 9-inch pie plate. Prebake and allow to cool.

FILLING

1. Preheat oven to 350 degrees F.

2. Combine the raisins, lemon juice and lemon zest. Allow to sit for 10 minutes.

3. Add the chopped nuts to raisin mix. Set aside.

4. Blend the oil, both sugars, cinnamon and salt together on medium-high speed until light and fluffy.

5. Add the eggs, one at a time, on medium speed until blended.

6. Using a wooden spoon, stir in the raisin mixture.

7. Spread the lemon-raisin mixture over the baked pie shell.

8. Bake for 35-40 minutes at 350 degrees F. The pie will be light gold in the middle and darker gold on the edges.

9. Cool completely on a wire rack before serving.

"To Kill for" Chocolate Pie

Ingredients

CRUST

1 single Basic Pie Crust *(pages 194-195)*

FILLING

4 ounces semisweet chocolate

½ cup canola oil

3 large eggs, at room temperature

1 cup granulated sugar

Important: Be sure to read the ingredients list on semisweet chocolate chips and semisweet solid bars for baking. Do not use brands that have butter fat, anhydrous butter, whey, lactose or any other dairy product.

8-12 SERVINGS

"To Kill for" Chocolate Pie

Directions

~⌒

CRUST

1. Make the pie crust. Place the crust into a 9-inch pie plate. Prebake and allow to cool.

FILLING

1. Preheat oven to 375 degrees F.

2. Melt the chocolate in a double boiler with the oil. Stir until blended. Remove from heat and let sit for 5 minutes.

3. Beat the egg and granulated sugar together with an electric mixer on medium until blended.

4. Add the chocolate mixture and mix on medium speed until blended.

5. Spread the chocolate mixture over the prepared pie shell.

6. Bake for 30 minutes at 375 degrees F. Reduce heat to 350 degrees F. and bake for 5-10 minutes more. The filling will set and form a crust.

7. Cool on a wire rack for ½ hour. Serve warm.

Basic Pie Crust

Ingredients

Single Crust

1½ cups unbleached white flour
1 pinch salt
⅓ cup canola oil
½ cup ice water

Double Crust

3 cups unbleached white flour
2 pinches salt
⅔ cup canola oil
1 cup ice water

Basic Pie Crust

Directions

1. Combine flour and salt. Blend.
2. Add the oil and blend until the mixture resembles course corn-meal.
3. Pour half of the ice water over the flour mixture and toss with a fork. Add water as needed to hold dough together.
4. On a lightly floured surface, knead the dough until it comes together.
5. Shape the dough into a ball *(or two balls if making the double crust)* and roll out. Fit the pie crust into a lightly greased 9-inch pie plate loosely and press against the sides. Trim the edges. Wrap in plastic wrap and keep refrigerated until needed.

TO PRE-BAKE

1. Preheat oven to 350 degrees F.
2. Pierce the bottom of the pie crust with a fork.
3. Bake for about 20 minutes at 350 degrees F. Pie shell will be golden brown.
4. Cool before filling.

Basic Tart Crust

Ingredients

Single Crust

1 cup unbleached white flour

3 tablespoons sugar

1 pinch salt

⅓ cup canola oil

1 tablespoon cold water

1 large egg yolk

Double Crust

2 cups unbleached white flour

⅓ cup sugar

2 pinches salt

⅔ cup canola oil

2 tablespoons cold water

2 large egg yolks

Basic Tart Crust

Directions

━━◇━━

1. Lightly grease a 9-inch tart pan with canola oil.
2. Combine flour, sugar and salt. Blend.
3. Add the oil and blend until the mixture resembles course corn-meal.
4. In a separate bowl whisk together the water and egg yolk.
5. Pour the egg mixture over the flour mixture and toss with a fork.
6. Press the dough evenly against the bottom and up the sides of the prepared pan.

TO PRE-BAKE

1. Preheat oven to 400 degrees F.
2. Pierce the bottom of the pie crust with a fork.
3. Bake for 15 minutes *(20 minutes for a crunchier tart crust)* at 400 degrees F. Tart shell will be golden brown.
4. Cool before filling.

VI
Puddings
&
Compotes
&
Mousse

Chocolate Mousse

Ingredients

¾ cup granulated sugar

½ cup unsweetened cocoa

¼ cup water

1 tablespoon instant coffee granules

5 large eggs, separated, at room temperature

1 pinch salt

2 tablespoons raspberry or strawberry liqueur

8 SERVINGS

Chocolate Mousse

Directions

1. Combine the sugar, cocoa, water, and coffee granules in a small sauce pan on medium heat for 3-4 minutes until the sugar dissolves and the mixture is smooth and thick.
2. In a small bowl beat the egg yolks with a fork. Add to the cocoa mixture and cook for 1 minute. Remove from heat and cool.
3. Beat the egg whites in an electric mixer on high speed until frothed. Add the salt and continue beating on high speed until soft peaks form.
4. Add the liqueur to the cooled cocoa mixture.
5. Using a spatula, gently fold the meringue into the cocoa mixture. Be sure to blend the mixture well without deflating the mousse.
6. Spoon into glass dessert dishes. Refrigerate for a minimum of 1 hour before serving. Mousse is best eaten the day it is prepared.

Chocolate Pudding

Ingredients

4 ounces semisweet chocolate

2 ounces unsweetened chocolate

2½ cups water

4 large egg yolks, at room temperature

1 cup granulated sugar

¼ cup unbleached white flour

3 tablespoons cornstarch

2 tablespoons water

2 teaspoons vanilla extract

Important: Be sure to read the ingredients list on semisweet chocolate chips and semisweet solid bars for baking. Do not use brands that have butter fat, anhydrous butter, whey, lactose or any other dairy product.

8 SERVINGS

Chocolate Pudding

Directions

1. Melt the two chocolates in a double boiler. Set aside.
2. In a medium saucepan heat the water over medium heat until it begins to boil.
3. Combine egg yolks, sugar, flour and cornstarch in a small bowl.
4. Add 2 tablespoons water to make a paste.
5. Add the boiling water to the paste, stirring vigorously with a whisk.
6. Transfer the cornstarch mixture back to the medium saucepan and heat on medium-low until it comes to a boil, stirring constantly. When the mixture comes to a boil, heat for 1 minute before removing from heat.
7. Add the melted chocolates and vanilla to the boiling mixture, stirring constantly until blended and smooth.
8. Spoon into glass dessert dishes. Cover and refrigerate until completely chilled before serving.

Crème de Cassis Pears

Ingredients

6 ripe but firm Bartlett pears, peeled with stems intact
2 cups red wine
2 whole cloves
2 cinnamon sticks
1 dash freshly ground black pepper
2 cups crème de cassis liqueur

6 SERVINGS

Crème de Cassis Pears

Directions

1. Preheat oven to 350 degrees F.
2. Place whole pears, red wine, whole cloves, cinnamon sticks and pepper in a large saucepan and bring to boil over medium heat.
3. Reduce heat and simmer for 15 minutes.
4. Transfer the pears to a small roasting pan with a slotted spoon.
5. Reserve the red wine mixture.
6. Pour the crème de cassis over the pears and place in oven.
7. Bake for 1 hour at 350 degrees F., basting every 10 minutes.
8. If the basting mixture runs low, stir in some of the reserved red wine mixture.
9. To serve, place pears on a platter and pour the crème de cassis used for basting over them.

English Trifle

Ingredients

CAKE

1 Yellow Cake recipe *(pages 84-85)*

FILLING

2 Lemon Custard recipes—use warm *(pages 222-223)*
1½ cups strawberry preserves
¾ cup apricot purée
2 cups mandarin oranges, drained
1 cup fresh strawberries, washed, sliced in half, stems
   removed
1 cup fresh or frozen blueberries
   *(Note: Any canned or fresh fruit can be used to make
   this trifle. Be creative!)*
½ cup sherry or rum

MAKES ABOUT 3 CUPS

English Trifle

Directions

ASSEMBLY

1. Cut the two cakes in half horizontally to make four thin cakes. Spread the strawberry preserves on one of the cakes and sandwich back together. Spread the apricot purée on the second cake and sandwich back together.

2. Cut the cakes into ¼-inch stripes.

3. Line the bottom of the trifle bowl with stripes from one of the cakes. Pour ¼ cup of the sherry or rum over the cake. Cover with the mandarin oranges. Be sure to line the edge of the bowl with the fruit so it can be seen from the outside. Cover the oranges with 1¼ cups of custard.

4. Repeat step 3 until all of the ingredients are used up. End with a layer of custard.

5. Cover and chill for 2 hours before serving.

6. Garnish with the fresh strawberries.

Steamed Chocolate Pudding

Ingredients

4 ounces semisweet chocolate
½ cup canola oil
1 cup unbleached white flour
1½ teaspoons baking powder
1 large egg, at room temperature
½ cup granulated sugar
½ cup boiling water
2 tablespoons vanilla extract

Important: Be sure to read the ingredients list on semisweet choco-late chips and semisweet solid bars for baking. Do not use brands that have butter fat, anhydrous butter, whey, lactose or any other dairy product.

6-8 SERVINGS

Steamed Chocolate Pudding

Directions

~⌒

1. Lightly grease a 1-quart steamed pudding mold.
2. Melt the chocolate in a double boiler with the oil. Stir until blended. Remove from heat.
3. Combine the flour and baking powder. Set aside.
4. Combine egg and sugar and blend with a fork.
5. Add the egg mixture to the chocolate mixture.
6. Gently fold in the flour mixture until blended.
7. Add the boiling water and vanilla to the batter and blend.
8. Pour the batter into the prepared pan. Seal shut. Set the mold on a wire rack in a large pot. Pour boiling water into the pot until it reaches half way up the sides of the mold.
9. Cover the pot and place on medium heat until the water starts to simmer. Steam the pudding for about 1½ hours or until the pudding sets. Add water as needed.
10. Remove the mold from the pot and invert the pudding on to a serving platter before removing the mold. Serve hot or at room temperature.

Westover's Baked Apple Pudding

Ingredients

FILLING

8 medium sized apples, peeled, cored and cut into ½-inch
  chunks
1 tablespoon canola oil
⅓ cup light brown sugar *(lightly packed)*
⅓ cup granulated sugar
2 tablespoons cornstarch
1 teaspoon nutmeg
1 teaspoon cinnamon
½ cup water

TOPPING

1½ cups unbleached white flour
¼ cup granulated sugar
1 teaspoon baking powder
1 pinch salt
⅔ cup orange juice
¼ cup canola oil

CUSTARD

1 Lemon Custard Recipe *(pages 222-223)*

8-10 SERVINGS

Westover's Baked Apple Pudding

Directions

~~

FILLING

1. Preheat oven to 350 degrees F.
2. Lightly grease a 2-quart casserole dish with canola oil.
3. Saute the apples in the oil in a large saucepan over medium heat until soft.
4. Add the sugars, cornstarch, nutmeg, cinnamon and water to the apples. Stir until blended.
5. Pour into prepared pan. Set aside.

TOPPING

1. Combine the flour, sugar, baking powder and salt in a large bowl.
2. Add the orange juice and oil to flour mixture and blend.
3. Spread the topping over the apple mixture.
4. Bake for 55-60 minutes at 350 degrees F. The top will be golden brown. The filling will be bubbly.
5. Serve hot with the warm custard.

VII

Frostings
&
Toppings
&
Fillings

Almond Custard Filling

Ingredients

3 tablespoons cornstarch
1 cup water
2 large eggs, at room temperature
¾ cup granulated sugar
1 pinch salt
2 tablespoons almond extract

2 CUPS

Almond Custard Filling

Directions

1. Dissolve the cornstarch in ½ cup water.
2. Add the eggs and whisk until blended.
3. Combine the ½ cup water, sugar and salt in a small sauce pan and heat until the sugar dissolves.
4. Combine the cornstarch mixture to the hot liquid, stirring constantly.
5. Add the almond extract, stirring constantly for about 3 or 4 minutes. The mixture will thicken. Continue to cook for 1 minute more, stirring constantly.
6. Remove the custard from heat and pour into a bowl through a sieve.
7. Allow the custard to cool in the bowl for 15 minutes before covering with plastic wrap.
8. Refrigerate for 2 hours before using.

Chocolate Frosting

Ingredients

2 cups confectioner's sugar
4 tablespoons unsweetened cocoa
2 tablespoons canola oil
5 tablespoons boiling water

2 CUPS

Chocolate Frosting

Directions

~⌒

1. Combine the sugar and cocoa in a small bowl.
2. Add the canola oil and blend.
3. GRADUALLY add the boiling water while whisking.
4. Add water until the desired consistency is attained.
5. If you add too much water and the frosting becomes too runny, add more confectioner's sugar.

Use as icing on your favorite brownie recipe or drizzle it over a cake.

Chocolate Icing

Ingredients

1½ cups semisweet chocolate
½ cup canola oil
²/₃ cup boiling water
1 teaspoon vanilla extract
1 cup confectioner's sugar *(sifted)*

Important: Be sure to read the ingredients list on semisweet chocolate chips and semisweet solid bars for baking. Do not use brands that have butter fat, anhydrous butter, whey, lactose or any other dairy product.

2½ CUPS

Chocolate Icing

Directions

1. Melt the chocolate in a double boiler with the oil. Stir until blended.
2. Remove from heat and stir in the water and vanilla.
3. Transfer chocolate mixture to a mixing bowl.
4. GRADUALLY add the sugar with an electric mixer on medium speed until smooth *(mixture will be runny)*.
5. Cover and refrigerate the icing for one hour before using.

Use as icing on your favorite brownie recipe or drizzle it over a cake.

Lemon Custard Filling

Ingredients

3 tablespoons cornstarch
1 cup water
2 large eggs, at room temperature
¾ cup granulated sugar
1 pinch salt
⅓ cup lemon juice

2 CUPS

Lemon Custard Filling

Directions

1. Dissolve the cornstarch in ½ cup water.
2. Add the eggs and whisk until blended. Set aside.
3. Combine the remaining ½ cup water, sugar and salt in a small sauce pan and heat until the sugar dissolves.
4. Combine the cornstarch mixture to the hot liquid, stirring constantly.
5. Add the lemon juice, stirring constantly for about 3 or 4 minutes. The mixture will thicken. Continue to cook for 1 minute more, stirring constantly.
6. Remove the custard from heat and pour into a bowl through a sieve.
7. Allow the custard to cool in the bowl for 15 minutes before covering with plastic wrap.
8. Refrigerate for 2 hours before using.

Mocha Jake's Sauce

Ingredients

1 cup boiling water
¾ cup unsweetened cocoa
¾ cup granulated sugar
1 tablespoon *(heaping)* instant coffee granules
1 teaspoon vanilla extract
1 teaspoon cinnamon
1 pinch salt

2½ CUPS

Mocha Jake's Sauce

Directions

1. In a medium sauce pan bring the water to a boil.
2. Combine the cocoa, sugar, coffee granules, vanilla, cinnamon and salt.
3. Add the cocoa mixture to the boiling water, stirring constantly for about 5 minutes. The mixture will thicken.
4. Remove the mixture from heat and pour into a bowl.
5. Allow the sauce to cool in the bowl for about 15 minutes before covering with plastic wrap.

Raspberry Sauce

Ingredients

1½ cups raspberries *(frozen or fresh)*
½ cup granulated sugar
¼ cup water
2 teaspoons cornstarch

¾ CUP

Raspberry Sauce

Directions

1. Combine the raspberries, sugar and water in a medium saucepan and cook over medium heat until the sugar dissolves. **DO NOT BOIL.**
2. Remove from heat and cool for 10 minutes.
3. Strain the raspberry mixture through a fine-mesh sieve to remove the seeds.
4. To thicken combine strained raspberry sauce and 1 teaspoon cornstarch in a medium sized saucepan over medium-high heat and bring to a boil.
5. To make a thicker sauce. Dissolve a second teaspoon of cornstarch in 2 tablespoons water and whisk into the boiling sauce.
6. Stir the sauce before using, as it will separate
7. Serve chilled.

Use as a complement to chocolate desserts or berry tarts.

Strawberry Sauce

Ingredients

1½ cups strawberries *(frozen or fresh)*
½ cup granulated sugar
2 teaspoons cornstarch
¼ cup water

¾ CUP

Strawberry Sauce

Directions

1. Combine the strawberries, sugar and water in a medium sauce-pan and cook over medium heat until the sugar dissolves. **DO NOT BOIL.**
2. Remove from heat and cool for 10 minutes.
3. Strain the strawberry mixture through a fine-mesh sieve to remove the seeds.
4. To thicken, combine strained raspberry sauce and 1 teaspoon cornstarch in a medium sized saucepan over medium-high heat and bring to a boil.
5. To make a thicker sauce, dissolve a second teaspoon of corn-starch in 2 tablespoons water and whisk into the boiling sauce.
6. Stir the sauce before using, as it will separate
7. Serve chilled.

Use as a complement to chocolate desserts or berry tarts.

Vanilla Custard Filling

Ingredients

3 tablespoons cornstarch

1 cup water

2 large eggs, at room temperature

¾ cup granulated sugar

1 pinch salt

1 tablespoon vanilla extract

2 CUPS

Vanilla Custard Filling

Directions

1. Dissolve the cornstarch in ½ cup water.
2. Add the eggs and whisk until blended. Set aside.
3. Combine the remaining ½ cup water, sugar and salt in a small sauce pan and heat until the sugar dissolves.
4. Combine the cornstarch mixture to the hot liquid, stirring constantly.
5. Add the vanilla extract, stirring constantly for about 3 or 4 minutes. The mixture will thicken. Continue to cook for 1 minute more, stirring constantly.
6. Remove the custard from heat and pour into a bowl through a sieve.
7. Allow the custard to cool in the bowl for about 15 minutes before covering with plastic wrap.
8. Refrigerate for 2 hours before using.

White Icing

Ingredients

3 large egg whites, at room temperature
2¼ cups sugar
1 cup boiling water
1 tablespoon light corn syrup
1 teaspoon vanilla extract

4 CUPS

White Icing

Directions

1. Beat the egg whites with an electric mixer on high speed until frothed. Add ¼ cup sugar and continue beating until the egg whites form soft peaks.
2. Combine the boiling water, remaining sugar and corn syrup in a large saucepan over medium heat.
3. Cook at a rolling boil, stirring constantly, for about 5 minutes or until the mixture reaches soft ball stage. *(To test for soft ball stage, drop a small amount of the mixture into a cold glass of water after it has cooked for about 5 minutes. If the drop forms into a soft ball, the mixture is ready. If using a candy thermometer, it will read 238 degrees F.)*
4. When the sugar mixture reaches soft ball stage, pour the mixture in a slow steady stream into the prepared egg whites with the mixer running continuously at medium-high speed. Add the vanilla when the mixture is completely blended.

Index

The Quick & Easy Organic Gourmet
Delicious, Healthy Meals Without Meat, Wheat, Dairy, or Sugar
LESLIE CERIER

For vegetarians, vegans, the allergy-stricken, and those with restricted diets, as well as those interested in food as a means for healing, this book offers mouthwatering combinations for cooking with organic foods. With scores of recipes for pastries, cookies, muffins, bread, casseroles, and more, Cerier demystifies the increasingly popular "ancient" grains–spelt, teff, kamut, and quinoa–that are more nutritious than wheat and far less likely to cause allergies.

Leslie Cerier is a chef, caterer, cooking teacher, and national authority on cooking with teff. She has written numerous articles on nutrition, cooking, and natural living for *Boston Line / Personal*, *Natural Health*, and local newspapers. She lives in Western Massachusetts.

$17.95 paper   ISBN 1-886449-00-7   7⅜ x 9¼   352 pages